MESSAGES FROM HEAVEN

MESSAGES

FROM

HEAVEN

What Jesus, Buddha, Moses,
and Muhammad Would Say Today

RYUHO OKAWA

IRH Press

IRH PRESS

New York . Tokyo

Distributed by Midpoint Trade Books. www.midpointtrade.com

Library of Congress Cataloging-in-Publication Data

ISBN 13: 978-1-941779-19-4

ISBN 10: 1-941779-19-0

Printed in China

Jacket Art and Design: Whitney Cookman

Book Design: Jennifer Daddio/Bookmark Design & Media Inc.

CONTENTS

PROLOGUE
My Life and Spiritual Messages

CHAPTER 1: JESUS CHRIST
Love Brings Us All Together

CHAPTER 2: SHAKYAMUNI BUDDHA
The Path to Enlightenment

CHAPTER 3: MOSES
Righteousness Must Prevail

CHAPTER 4: MUHAMMAD
Be Humble before God

EPILOGUE
Eternal Truths for a Happy World

My Life and Spiritual Messages

HOW I STARTED RECEIVING SPIRITUAL MESSAGES

It was March 23, 1981, when I received my first spiritual message from Heaven. It was just a few days before my graduation from university, right before I began working for a trading firm. For the previous few months, I'd become deeply introspective. On that fine afternoon in early spring, I was looking deep inside my mind and reflecting on my life up to that point. As I looked back, I realized that I had made many mistakes and caused a lot of trouble for people around me. I hadn't appreciated how much my parents had done for me throughout my life. I had sometimes thought or acted wrongly. I had thoughtlessly said and done things that hurt people's feelings, and even though they had been unintentional, I regretted them. I carefully examined my words, actions, and thoughts, and one by one, I repented them.

As I was reflecting, a warm feeling welled up within my chest, and I felt keenly that I had been living life as a false self. It was then that I felt a premonition that something was going to happen. I could not see anyone in the room with me, but I could sense that someone was near me, trying to tell me something. I had always believed in the existence of spiritual beings, but I had never expected that I would experience a spiritual phenomenon myself.

I felt an urge to write something, so I picked up a pencil and some blank index cards that were lying nearby. I waited, pencil in hand. Then suddenly, my hand began to move as if it had a life of its own. It wrote "Good News" on the first card. Then it wrote "Good News" on a second card, and then on a third card, too. My hand continued to write the same words over and over again on new cards, until finally I said, "I understand the 'Good News' part. Could you tell me something other than that?" But my hand just continued to write "Good News." That was all that happened that day, but I had a strong sense of anticipation that something more was going to follow. "Good News" is the literal meaning of the Christian word "gospel," and this divine revelation was telling me that something good was about to happen.

Eventually, I learned that the spirit who was sending me these messages was named Nikko; Nikko had been one of the six senior disciples of the thirteenth-century Buddhist priest Nichiren. After about a week, Nichiren himself started sending me messages by automatic writing. Soon I started to receive messages from other spirits as well, but most of the time, it was Nichiren who communicated with me and answered my questions. I didn't even have to put my questions into words: the moment I wondered about something, the answer would immediately come to me. This was undoubtedly a peculiar experience, and I wondered how it would turn out, so I kept records of every spiritual conversation I had so that I could keep track of how it progressed.

For several months, these conversations continued to take place through automatic writing, but in July, the spirits began to use my vocal cords to speak. I couldn't write fast enough to capture everything they were telling me, and because they wanted me to convey their messages more directly and freely, I became able to speak their words. It was indeed a mystical experience.

At this stage, my father, Saburo Yoshikawa, who had always had a strong interest in spirituality, began to join me in these question-and-answer sessions with the spirits; he and I would both ask questions, and the spirits would answer using my vocal cords. My father thought that we should keep word-for-word records of the spirits' messages, so we began to tape-record and transcribe our question-and-answer sessions.

I was receiving many messages from different spirits who all had unique personalities of their own. I summoned the same spirits multiple times over the course of several years to confirm whether their individual characters and the contents of their messages were consistent. I would summon a spirit, record his or her messages, and then wait for one or two years before recording that spirit's messages again. We recorded these messages for four or five years and found that their contents and the characteristics of the spirits stayed consistent. For example, we found that the individual character of Nichiren remained the same. The level of his messages was always very high, and what he said was profound that only a priest with a high level of awareness could have said such things.

In this way, my father and I compared the messages and confirmed the individual character of all the spirits, including their habits and patterns of speech. Eventually, we published our transcriptions as books to prove that spiritual beings with unique personalities exist. These books eventually formed the foundation of our spiritual movement's mission.

MY LIFE BEFORE AND AFTER I BEGAN RECEIVING SPIRITUAL MESSAGES

My parents were both deeply religious people, and I was educated in a religious environment from a young age, so I had the kind of foundation that led me to accept a spiritual perspective on life. My father was very curious about spiritual matters, and I grew up listening to his stories about the spiritual phenomena he had seen. He used to visit religious organizations and spiritual leaders, and whenever he heard about a supernatural phenomenon, he would go and see it for himself. He would even stay up all night on the chance of seeing a ghost. He was a lot more into spirituality than I was, and I often tried to persuade him not to get so immersed in such matters.

Despite my father's interest in spirituality, my upbringing was quite conventional and centered on school. I focused mainly on accumulating knowledge and experience in the physical world. So until I was in my teens, I was, for the most part, left-brain-oriented. That is to say, I developed the "calculating brain" and the "language brain" more than the right brain—the "image brain." Spiritually sensitive people typically interact with the spirits using the right brain. Usually, people like me are unsusceptible to spiritual revelations, because spiritual ability is incompatible with the skills that are cultivated by training the left brain. But I was innately artistic, literary, and emotionally sensitive. Although I don't paint, I often use the right brain to draw a picture in my head and create various images and visions. Then I use the left brain to put those images into words or actualize them in the physical world. I ended up developing both spiritual powers and worldly skills so that I became sort of "ambidextrous."

Still, up until I started receiving spiritual messages, most of my efforts in life had gone into preparing to be successful in the terms of this world, not the spiritual world. I was living a worldly lifestyle and never imagined that the time would come when it would be my job to teach spiritual Truths.

At that time, two preoccupations troubled me most. The first was related to the realization of my personal goals. I felt very strongly that I wanted to develop my abilities fully and live the kind of life I felt I deserved. I had a very powerful desire to live my ideals, but things did not always turn out as I would have liked them to. As a result, I suffered a lot of disappointment and felt as if an irrational force were placing roadblocks in front of me.

My other preoccupation had to do with love. It is only natural for human beings to want to be loved by others. I believe that everybody is the same in this respect; we very often suffer, particularly in adolescence, because we are unable to receive love. I paid little regard to all the things that other people had done for me; instead, I often felt frustrated, disappointed, and unhappy because I was unable to attain something or to receive what I expected from others. What's more, I felt that it was quite normal to feel that way.

I was very sensitive and prone to negativity. When I received praise, I couldn't rejoice or appreciate it, but the slightest insult would pierce me like a thorn and rankle me for years. We often say things without any intention of hurting anyone, but I used to take people's casual remarks to heart and hold on to them for years, as though every criticism were a dagger that just stayed in my heart. I was suffering from an immense sense of failure; I felt miserable and worthless and wondered why I had been born into this world. When I looked at the world around me, I saw so much evil and contradiction that I was filled with righteous indignation at all the injustice. I could not find it within me to forgive those who had committed wrongdoings; instead, I felt an overwhelming desire to bring them to justice.

Then, just before I began to receive spiritual messages, I underwent a period of introspection. I had felt a strong desire to set aside quiet time to look within myself, in silence. As I reflected back on my life, the door to my subconscious gradually began to open, and eventually I came into direct contact with the spirit world. Initially, I felt conflicted and resisted the idea of connecting with the spirit world. On one hand, the messages I was receiving felt like a calling—an invitation from Heaven. I felt that my situation and experience were like those of the prophets in the Old Testament whom God had called to service. On the other hand, I felt confused about why I had to go into that world, and I thought that I did not have enough spiritual training or knowledge to truly answer the call. I really wasn't sure if I was capable or good enough to be a spiritual leader. I couldn't help but feel that there were others who were more cut out for spiritual leadership than I was.

In short, I had no idea how to cope with what happened to me. But in the following years, I read widely on spirituality and realized that there were others who had had similar experiences. One was Mother Teresa of Calcutta, who one day heard the voice of Jesus Christ when she was traveling on a train and realized her life's mission. After that, she began her great work in India.

Gradually, I became used to having daily communication with the spirits. And then I received a message that had a profound effect on my perspective. During the initial period of automatic writing, I had asked Nichiren what my mission on Earth was—what I had been sent here to do. He answered, "Love, Nurture, and Forgive." I considered the meaning of this simple message for several months until finally I understood that it summed up the core of the philosophy I was to develop and the core of my work in this world.

I continued to ponder this single line of text for almost three years while I worked at a major Japanese trading company. I kept repeating these words to myself as I tried to figure out what to do with my life. I gradually came to realize that the three words of Nichiren's message—love, nurture, and forgive—all indicated a certain direction. To love people, to nurture them, and to forgive them all involved a proactive approach on my end, without thinking of any return for myself. In other words, they represented a form of altruism.

These three words from Nichiren spurred me to make a complete, 180-degree change of perspective. I realized that the happiness I had been pursuing my whole life was not real happiness after all. I had thought that happiness was something given by others. I had thought that I was happy when I received praise and admiration from others. But Nichiren's words were telling me to do the opposite of receiving from others.

I looked back on my life and asked myself whether I had ever actually loved anybody, or whether I had even tried to love others. I could only think of a few instances of having genuinely given love to another. On the contrary, I began to realize how often I had been the receiver of love—in particular, how much others had done for me over the years. I began to recognize just how much I owed my parents, friends, and teachers for all they had done to help me. I realized that I had been able to devote myself to my studies because of their support and the environment they had created for me. And as I studied, I had mostly thought of myself. I had expected something—personal gain or recognition—in return for my effort.

I began to create a "love balance sheet," a mental list of everything that others had done for me and everything I had done for others. I listed things that I had done for others in the "assets" column and things that others had done to help me in the "liabilities" column. It was surprising to learn just how much I had received from others and how little I had done for them in return. When I added everything up, I deeply regretted the way I had been living and knew I needed to become a new person. When I was faced with this truth, I began to think that there must be a far greater kind of happiness than the kind I had been trying to achieve by just fulfilling my wants.

I realized that we experience happiness when we feel that we have grown and when we increase our presence in the world. The wish to be recognized and appreciated must come from the desire to grow, but taking love from others cannot fulfill this desire. That would be merely an attempt to fill in the parts of ourselves that we feel are missing. Self-development in the truest sense is planting a part of your own soul, spirit, mind, or heart in others. It is about having a positive influence on others through your way of living or thinking.

We generally think that we lose something when we give and

gain something when we receive. But from a spiritual perspective, the more we give, the more we grow. The true path to self-development does not lie in defending our own interests. True happiness can only be found by understanding our true worth as human beings and by being of service to others.

This was what I found when I contemplated the phrase, "Love, Nurture, and Forgive." As I continued to contemplate, I became convinced that love has different developmental stages. And then, when I was about twenty-seven years old, I managed to develop these three simple words into the "Stages of Love" philosophy.* When this philosophy took a clear shape, it marked the beginning of the next phase of my own spiritual development. I began to contemplate how to put this philosophy into practice, and after another three years, I felt ready to go out and actually teach spiritual Truths publicly.

RECORDING AND EDITING SPIRITUAL MESSAGES
WHILE WORKING FULL-TIME IN BUSINESS

While I was receiving spiritual messages from Nichiren and other divine spirits, I had a full-time job at a large Japanese trading firm where I was often quite overwhelmed by the work. Throughout this period, my father, Saburo Yoshikawa, was a great source of strength to me. He worked hard to compile the spiritual messages I received, arrange them into book form, and find a publisher for them.

My father used to travel to the area where I lived and stay in a hotel there, and we would record the spiritual messages in his hotel.

---

* See Ryuho Okawa, "The River of God's Love" in *The Laws of the Sun* (New York: IRH Press, 2013) for detailed explanation of the Stages of Love philosophy.

We also recorded some of them when I traveled back to my hometown of Tokushima on weekends, summer vacations, New Year's holidays, and other holidays. I would go back home so frequently—once or twice a month—that my colleagues would ask, "You go back home so often. Are you seeing someone in your hometown?" or "Are you going back there to find a wife?" They used to tease me, saying, "Wow, you must be desperate if you have to go home so often to find a wife." So I went along with them and said, "Yeah, I am really popular in my hometown. It's really hard to turn down everyone's offers." But actually, I was busy "seeing" the spirits. I was "seeing" someone, but it wasn't a living person, nor was it always a female. I was going back home to "see" ghosts.

At the time, I was living in a company dormitory, and my father used to call me to discuss editorial matters. My colleagues thought we were talking about my marriage arrangements, so they used to say, "You're setting up another date? You must be really popular." But actually, we were discussing whether to delete or edit certain contents or leave them the way they were. People around me thought it was strange that my father called me so often, but it was because I was working on these books while trying to hide what I was doing.

In this way, I continued to publish books of spiritual messages. But these books were different from anything I had read in the past, so as I published them, I was also studying the opinions of the spirits. All their opinions contained some truth, but some also had unique and odd ideas. I was surprised to find that even among the spirits, opinions differ. The spirits would even argue with one another due to their differences of opinion. For this reason, I was especially careful to empirically check, confirm, and verify what they said to see whether they were right or wrong.

I was developing my own philosophy at the same time, but I thought that if I wrote a book about my own ideas, it would be difficult to then publish spiritual messages from a variety of spirits who had different opinions and thoughts. So I decided to publish the spiritual messages first, to prove the existence of the spirit world, and to introduce my own thoughts and philosophy later on.

It was extremely difficult to record and publish my spiritual messages, because no one understood what we were doing. Even if people firmly believe in the existence of the spirit world and spirits, they usually refrain from talking about these things in public. Because these things are not taught in school and usually are not related to people's work in society, they do not talk about them openly. Some might talk about them at church or at other religious services, but people usually don't discuss spiritual matters at work. It was in these circumstances that I was initially publishing the spiritual messages that I received from Heaven.

At work, I was surrounded by people who denied that such a thing was possible, so I had no one to talk to about what I was doing. But my parents gave me full support, which provided me with a certain sense of stability when I began my mission. I appreciate that my parents were religious and believed 100 percent in the existence of the other world. I am really grateful that my family was so understanding of spiritual Truths. It would have been much more difficult if the members of my family did not believe in spirits or the other world.

Nevertheless, this period of time was extremely painful for me. After a few years of working in two worlds like this, I had reached the point in my career at which I was approaching middle management. The path to promotion lay before me. I retained a strong ambition to advance in the business world and achieve personal success, but I also realized that I could not allow things to go on the way they were. I had to find some way of accomplishing the special mission I knew I had been given. These two paths were not compatible, and that caused a conflict within me. Part of my problem was fear of the unknown.

Would people really understand what I was about to begin? I struggled with the problem of how to go about spreading the knowledge I was gaining. I knew I wanted to create some kind of organization based on all I had been told, but I didn't know how to begin.

The situation came to a head shortly before my thirtieth birthday. The divine spirits who had been talking to me sent me a pivotal message, "Now is the time to move." Hearing this, I finally made up my mind to give notice to my company. I was determined to stand on my own two feet and live in the Truths. By then, we had already published five or six books; we were publishing new compilations of spiritual messages every two months. This was when I decided to leave my company and to found the spiritual organization that would become Happy Science.

CONVEYING THE WORDS OF SPIRITS: MEDIUMS, PROPHETS, AND TEACHERS

When people hear about someone conveying the words of spirits, they often think of it as just a psychic phenomenon. But those who can channel spirits usually fall into one of two categories: mediums or prophets.

When the spirit comes into the body of an ordinary psychic medium, the medium goes into a trance and later cannot recall what the spirit said. For example, when a shaman calls on the spirits, the shaman loses consciousness because the shaman's soul leaves the body when the spirit enters it. To speak through a psychic medium, a spirit has to possess the medium's entire body. Because the medium's spiritual power is much weaker than that of the spirits, the spirits can control the medium completely; the medium simply becomes a vehicle for conveying their words and is incapable of offering his or her own opinions.

This same phenomenon occurs in people who have been diagnosed with multiple personality disorder. All of a sudden, the person can become a completely different character and go by a completely different name. In some cases, it can be several months before the person's original character returns. It's likely that people with multiple personality disorder are actually being possessed by different spirits with different personalities. Psychic mediums and shamans are different from people with multiple personality disorder in that they can control this phenomenon: they can call the spirits using their own free will and allow the spirits to temporarily possess them.

Prophets, by contrast, are able to hear the words of God or see images of God while retaining their own consciousness. Many prophets merely receive revelations, see words, or hear voices, and do not offer a large volume of teachings. Instead, they receive a message from God that instructs them to do something specific during occasional turning points. For instance, there was the Prophecy of Fatima, during which the Virgin Mary appeared and made three predictions. Usually, prophets are only given a very small amount of spiritual information.

Then there are spiritual teachers. Spiritual teachers can preach their own unique, original teachings and possess an ability beyond that of prophets. This is a rare and exceptional case in which the spiritual status of the person living on Earth is superior to that of the spirits who are sending messages to him. Jesus and the Buddha, for example, were neither mediums nor prophets, but teachers. Their teachings did not simply convey the words of other spirits. They received messages and heard the voices of many different divine spirits, but they delivered their own teachings based on their own free will. They could preach a variety of teachings because they had the spiritual power to receive messages from a variety of divine spirits.

I am neither a medium nor a prophet, but rather a spiritual teacher like Jesus and the Buddha. When a spirit enters my body,

I retain my own consciousness. My soul remains in my body the entire time the spirit is speaking through me. It is like having two souls (spirits) inside my body. So I am able to hear the messages of the spirits, ask questions, and listen to the answers as myself. I can play two roles at the same time—I can ask questions and answer them. This is how I conduct my spiritual message sessions.

The reason I can do this is simply that I am very spiritually powerful. My own spirit-body is so strong that when another spirit enters my body, it can't control my body completely, nor can it push my own spirit-body away. In some cases, it is possible for me to receive spiritual messages from several spirits at the same time because my spiritual ability allows me to stay in control of the situation.

When I first began publishing my spiritual messages in the 1980s, my publisher thought that the spirits were more valuable than I was—he figured that I was just a medium. I knew that sometimes spirits are more valuable than the medium that conveys their messages, so I could understand why my publisher felt that way about me. I also knew that it could be very difficult to get a book published in the first place, so I decided to let go and let the publisher present the books in a way that highlighted the spirits rather than me.

Later on, though, I started publishing books that introduced my own philosophies and thoughts; I then became known as a religious leader. The ideas and opinions of the spirits had helped me construct the early foundations of my philosophies, but after I began to put my own philosophy together, I made it clear that I was a religious figure rather than a medium.

HOW SPIRITUAL COMMUNICATION WORKS

To this day, I still communicate with the spirits on a daily basis. Contacting a spirit that I would like to talk to is like making a telephone call. When I call them, they answer my call right away, and they also "call me"—that is, they come to talk to me—if they have something they want to tell me. I can communicate with the spirits no matter where I am or what time of the day it is, since the spirit world doesn't have the same concepts of time and physical distance as we have in this world.

When I communicate with spirits, I begin by concentrating my mind into a place of calm and peacefulness. If your mind is constantly wavering or preoccupied with worries, or if you feel tired or frustrated, you cannot communicate with heavenly spirits. You must have a calm and peaceful mind like the quiet surface of a lake. When I concentrate my mind and attain a peaceful state of mind, I can contact the spirit world in one or two seconds.

I can also talk to spirits by way of telepathy without even having to summon them. I talk to them just like you would engage in conversation with a physical person. Ordinary people would not be able to bear living this way. I am sure that most people would be scared if spirits appeared before them. It would be jarring to have spirits come into your room, say something to you, and leave as an ordinary part of your daily life. But I am used to constantly having sprits around me, because I have been living like this for the last thirty years. I think it is a rare life experience.

I used to only speak with the spirits of great figures, but today, the guardian spirits* of the people I know come and see me every day and give me a piece of their mind. I only allow certain spirits to talk to me. For example, the guardian spirits of the executive members of our organization often come to tell me their opinions.

---

* Guardian spirits are a part of our souls, or a part of the consciousness of the people living on Earth; they reflect our thoughts and personalities. Everyone has a guardian spirit that provides spiritual guidance throughout the person's life. For more information, see Ryuho Okawa, *The Laws of the Sun* (New York: IRH Press, 2013).

The guardian spirits are very honest; they tell me what they are really thinking. So when the guardian spirits of the executives come to speak to me, I listen. Even if the executives themselves deny that they are thinking about the things that their guardian spirits have told me, things usually unfold in the way that their guardian spirits have indicated. The guardian spirits usually tell me ahead of time what their physical counterparts are planning to do or say in the near future, even before the people living on Earth become aware of their own true intentions. But what the guardian spirits say are the people's true thoughts, and the people's actions and words originate from the guardian spirits. Since the guardian spirit constantly sends inspiration to the person living on Earth, the person begins to think and act according to the opinions of the guardian spirit. On the other hand, guardian spirits do sometimes exaggerate, so I take that into account.

When I receive and convey messages from spirits, I let the spirits speak through me, but at the same time, I listen to their opinions and evaluate them as a spirit judge. I'm responsible for ascertaining which god or spirit is speaking, interpreting the message I'm receiving, and passing judgment on the contents of the message. So when I give spiritual messages, I have three different roles: conveying the words of the spirit, watching myself as I convey the spiritual message, and watching the whole scene objectively. I have an objective perspective that lets me observe the situation and listen to the interview, thinking such things as, "I would ask these questions instead." If I wanted to, I could ask questions and answer them, but I don't do that because I think that would be too confusing for the audience.

I have summoned a lot of foreign spirits, and many people wonder how I can communicate with spirits who speak foreign languages, so let me explain how this works. I lived in New York for about a year, at a time when my spiritual eyes had opened and I was able to communicate with spirits. When you live in foreign countries, you come into contact with many foreign spirits, but to tell you the truth, it's difficult to communicate with them. When ordinary people die, their consciousness remains the same, so they can only speak the language that they spoke when they were alive. So unless you speak the same language, it's quite difficult to communicate with their spirit.

But spirits from higher worlds—beings known as angels, bodhisattvas, or *tathagatas**—have much more developed spiritual abilities. For instance, Jesus Christ spoke a Hebrew dialect (Aramaic) when he was alive, but today, after two thousand years, Christianity has spread to the English-speaking world, and native English speakers read the Bible and pray in English. So if Jesus were only able to speak and understand Hebrew, he wouldn't be able to do his job. There are Christians all over the world, so to do his job, Jesus needs to be able to understand prayers in many different languages. Like Jesus, divine spirits in the higher dimensions have abilities that transcend language barriers. Language is simply a verbal manifestation of our will or our thoughts, and spirits in the higher dimensions can read people's thoughts before they come out as words. That's why they can understand and communicate with people who speak different languages.

Let me give you an example of what happens when foreign spirits send their messages to me. When Confucius sent his messages to me, he spoke in Chinese for the first fifteen minutes. But after a

---

* Bodhisattvas are equivalent to angels in Christianity. They work to spread God's Truths and offer people salvation. Like the word *bodhisattva*, *tathagata* is a Buddhist term that means "coming from the Eternal Truths" or "embodying the absolute Truths of God." Tathagatas are the equivalent of archangels in Christianity and are sometimes referred to as Great Guiding Spirits of Light. See Ryuho Okawa, *The Nine Dimensions* (New York: IRH Press, 2012).

while, my linguistic center started to focus, and I started receiving his will—his meaning, or what he was trying to say. Then I was able to translate what he wanted to say into my native language of Japanese, just like simultaneous interpretation. I did the same thing with Moses and Jesus Christ. They have a bit of an accent, but their message comes out in Japanese. I can decipher the essence or the basis of the ideas without using words.

So whatever the spirit's language is, I can understand what the spirit is going to say even before he or she starts speaking. Even before the spiritual interview begins, I can understand what the spirit is going to say in an instant. I can grasp the whole picture as a concept. And then it's only a matter of how to express it. I can now understand various languages more easily than I used to, because my translation faculties have improved. But basically, I hear words that have yet to become words.

Even before words were created, human beings were able to communicate with one another. Words came into existence and developed gradually over time. I think that the modern languages and grammars that we use today probably developed only in the last one thousand years or so. But before that, human beings still shared their ideas with one another.

Thought comes before speech. Before you speak, you have a thought that you want to communicate. That thought passes through the circuits of your brain and comes out as words in the language you speak. I can grasp most of the spirit's intended meaning even before the thought circulates through my brain and becomes speech. However, I still feel responsible for expressing the spirit's idea in a way that accords with his or her own will as much as possible.

I conduct readings not only with terrestrial human beings, but also with extraterrestrial beings. This is probably an even more difficult concept for people to grasp. There are words that I just cannot translate into the languages of Earth. So I grasp the idea coming from the soul of the extraterrestrial being and try to communicate that. This is probably closer to telepathy; it is the ability to read their minds.

ENLIGHTENING PEOPLE ABOUT THE TRUTHS OF THE SPIRIT WORLD

I began my mission to spread the Truths at the age of twenty-four, when divine spirits started sending me messages from Heaven. These spiritual messages were the starting point of my activities and of the spiritual movement that has now spread around the world.

These days, I conduct my spiritual message sessions in an interview format in front of an audience in the hope of raising people's awareness about the existence of spirits and the spirit world. For me, it is obvious that the spirit world exists, but a lot of people still doubt its existence. About ten years after my first book of spiritual messages (*The Spiritual Message of Nichiren,* published in 1985), I stopped publishing spiritual messages and started publishing my own philosophies and teachings. More recently, I began to feel that the time had come again when we must prove that the spirit world really exists. So in 2009, I started conducting spiritual message sessions in public and publishing them, and this time, I have also included my own comments to introduce my views to the world.

I am sure that many readers who believe in the existence of the spirit world have a difficult time convincing others of its reality. But the truth is the truth, and no one can deny the truth. The spirit world and the spirits do indeed exist. This will become 100 percent clear to everyone after they die. We only have a grace period of several decades while we live on this earth; then everyone must face the final conclusion. No matter how much people deny the spirit world, it is a fact and truth. It exists, and those who believe in the spirits and the other world are the ones who have it right.

In this book, you will hear from spirits who lived on Earth a few thousand years ago. Their messages, however, are not old at all, but up to date. If the spirits were to come down in front of you, you would probably ask many of the questions that I have asked them. So I believe that you can experience these messages as if the spirits were talking directly to you right now.

In publishing these spiritual messages, I have slightly edited or changed some of the spirits' words. Otherwise, the messages are basically transcripts of what the spirits said in an actual conversation. In that sense, this book is proof that the spirit world exists.

For those who are new to my teachings, this book will help you see things from a new spiritual perspective. If you find this book helpful and would like to learn more, I recommend that you read some of the many books of my own teachings that I have published.

In addition, based on my experience, it is very important that you have someone in your family who shares your spiritual beliefs. If you can lead your own family to this path of Truth, you can start creating a better world. So I hope that you will read this book and start conveying the Truths to people around you.

It is my sincere wish that this book's spiritual messages will serve as a useful reference to you in your efforts to understand the Truths. I will be very happy if you can deepen your understanding of these messages and shine a new light in the world.

CHAPTER 1

JESUS CHRIST

Love Brings Us All Together

THE LIFE OF JESUS CHRIST*

Over the course of history, many great figures have emerged across religions and cultures to spread God's teachings for humanity. Every several hundred or several thousand years, God sends envoys from Heaven to create a foundation for the world's various civilizations and cultures. These men and women are extraordinary people who actualize God's teachings on Earth and eventually become the heart of their civilization.

Before Jesus Christ's birth, during the first century BCE, there was a widespread belief among Israelites in prophecies that foretold the emergence of a Messiah who would be born among the people of Israel. The prophecies foretold that the Messiah would establish a kingdom of God on Earth and would be crucified and resurrected. Many sects of Judaism had formed by this time. For example, the Pharisees preached strict adherence to the Ten Commandments, and the Sadducees represented the conservative majority. Jesus of Nazareth was born to parents in the Essene sect, which believed in and waited for the coming of the Messiah.

When Jesus was born, his father, Joseph, was thirty-six years old, and his mother, Mary, was seventeen. Many Christians believe in the virgin birth of Jesus, which is similar to the Buddhist belief that Shakyamuni Buddha was born from the armpit of Queen Maya. However, the story of Jesus's virgin birth was a creation of later Christians who wanted to convey their sense of Jesus's god-like standing and encourage people to believe that Jesus was the Messiah. In reality, Jesus was conceived the same way that every-

---

* The majority of this section was written through automatic writing. I cannot attest to the accuracy of its contents, but I have conveyed the information that I found in Heaven.

one else is conceived. But it is true that three wise men foresaw the Messiah's birth and followed a star into Judea to find him.

By the time Jesus was seven years old, an angel had already visited him. As a small child, he already possessed the gifts of spiritual speech, spiritual sight (clairvoyance), and spiritual hearing (clairaudience). At this young age, an angel would enter his body and enable him to hold eloquent discussions about the Hebrew Bible. The members of his community were amazed by his precociousness, and by the time he was ten years old, rumors that he was a child prodigy had spread widely. The elder Essene leaders realized that Jesus must be the Messiah that the Hebrew prophets had foretold. They took care to protect him from persecution by other sects and provided him with a good education.

Today, practically nothing is known about Jesus's young adulthood, because accounts of this stage of his life have been excised from the original Bible. I have discovered through my spiritual research that Jesus was given an elite religious education. His education included travels to places such as Egypt, where he spent approximately one year when he was thirteen, accompanied by a young Essene minister. There he learned about the various religions that existed in that region.

Then at the age of sixteen, he went to west India for a year and a half with several Jewish elders. In India, he learned traditional methods of yogic meditation and studied Buddhist scriptures. He also learned the skill of materialization; that is, he learned to use his willpower and the mystical power of prayer to create miracles in the physical world. While studying under a mystic named Manitula, he learned how to materialize bread and fish from thin air. And finally, on a philosophical level, he was captivated by Buddhist teachings of altruism and the Buddhist concept of making offerings.

When Jesus was twenty-one, he set out on another journey, this time to Persia. He learned the Zoroastrian concept of the dualism of good and evil and studied teachings about the Ahura Mazda, the supreme god of Zoroastrianism. But he could not fully reconcile himself with the Zoroastrian emphasis on fire-worship.

It was at the age of twenty-five that Jesus began to study the Hebrew Bible intently. Then, at twenty-seven, he began to practice meditation and austerity in a cave in Qumran near the Dead Sea. He spent three years practicing this discipline while he contemplated and built the framework of his teachings. One of El Cantare's brother souls, Hermes, taught Jesus about love, and this teaching had a strong impact on Jesus's spiritual awakening. Love became the essence of Jesus's teachings and later was the key to the worldwide dissemination of Christianity. From Buddhism, Jesus adopted the concept of karma, which teaches that we reap what we sow. He was certain that this was a valuable teaching. But he kept his main focus on the teachings of love because he felt that Buddhism was lacking in these teachings. From the yogis, he adopted the practice of spiritual power, which later helped him awaken his people, and from Zoroastrianism, he adopted the concept of driving out evil. As he integrated these various teachings, his core philosophy gradually began to take shape.

When Jesus was thirty years old, Archangel Gabriel, appeared before him during his meditation in the cave. Gabriel brought him this message: "You must return to Nazareth now. On your journey home, you will see a man giving baptisms on the shore of the Jordan River. This man is the famous John the Baptist. You will meet him, and this encounter will mark the beginning of your ministry on Earth. You must then set out to gather disciples. You will have twelve disciples. They will become the twelve apostles, the core disciples to whom you will spread your teachings."

We all know about what Jesus taught from then on, because

most of his teachings were eventually recorded in the Bible. Though his ministry only lasted three years, he had developed his teachings over the course of the previous twenty-three years, beginning at the age of seven. His teachings were profound and universal and inspired countless people with awe. When he died on a cross in Golgotha at the young age of thirty-three, he did not die in vain, for his death shaped the history of the world for the next two thousand years.

A MESSAGE FROM JESUS CHRIST

I. God Loves All People Without Discrimination

HATRED AND LOVE

Hatred and love are two basic human emotions. Because they seem to be on opposite ends of the emotional spectrum, they are commonly seen as two separate things, but in truth, hatred and love share the same foundation: the principle of love. Human love is the result of a total acceptance of the principle of love, while hatred is born of the rejection of this principle. Our rejection or acceptance of the principle of love is the only thing that sets these two emotions apart.

It is love's nature to keep circulating through the world. People only feel hatred when the natural flow of love has become plugged up. To allow love to flow again, we just have to pull out the plug.

We feel hatred when other people are not the way we want them to be or do not behave as we wish they would. Hatred arises when we feel angry that we cannot control others as we would like to. But at the end of the day, hatred is just another form of the natural desire for love. People who hate want to be loved, respected, and valued. They are starving for love but are not strong enough to give love to others.

By contrast, those with love do not seek anything—they only give. They keep giving and giving endlessly. They are able to do this because they are so aware of the many blessings God has given them. They want to share God's love with others because they realize that God has given them so much, and they want to keep God's love flowing.

Human love comes from the gratitude we feel when we realize that we have been blessed with everything. It is this realization that inspires us to give love to others. So I ask those of you who are burning with the flames of hatred right now to place your hands over your heart and ask yourselves whether you have gratitude. Are you grateful for all that God has given you? Do you feel thankful to all those who have helped you through life? Remember, a thankless heart is a heart devoid of love.

All of us should give love to others as often as possible, because God has already given each one of us everything we need. It is not in our true nature as humans to disregard God's blessings; it is not in our true nature to keep hungering for new things and demanding, "Do this for me. Do that for me."

Deeds that come from love are truly beautiful. Hatred not only harms others but also desecrates the sanctity of our divine nature. Therefore, we should cast all hatred out of us.

In this world of diverse people, it is impossible to control everyone as we please. Even God, the almighty, never forces His preferences onto anyone. God gives us the freedom to think on our own, speak our own words, and behave according to our own will. Even if we behave in a way that God would not approve or adopt a way of thinking that God dislikes, God forgives us for those mistakes; God supplies sunshine and warmth unconditionally to everyone, like the sun. God never stops nourishing us with clouds of rain and fields of grain.

If God forgives sinners, what gives us any right to judge them? We do not have any right to pass judgment on others. If we loathe being judged, then we must never judge others. We should never label anyone as evil. We should never label anyone as wrong. We should understand that God will keep nourishing them in just the same way that God nourishes everyone else.

God never plays favorites, either. God would never provide a better harvest to people who have been good than to people who have behaved badly. He would never send rain showers only upon the good and deny them to the bad. God never plays favorites. We should never think that God did not save a man from death because he may have lived a wrongful life. God will keep nourishing those who have committed wrong deeds, had evil thoughts, and said wrongful words.

We should all give more thought to the reason God never plays favorites: There is never a person who is completely evil. No one is a complete wrongdoer, and no one is ever a complete sinner. When people do wrong, they are acting defensively, out of fear of being hurt. And then we become defensive because we are afraid that they will hurt us; we may criticize them and put them down with the idea that such behaviors will protect us. But this is not something that God would approve.

So when people act hatefully toward you, answer them with love. When they throw anger your way, respond with a smile. When they hurl violent words at you, respond with silence. This is the way we should practice God's love.

LOVING NO MATTER WHAT

I would like people to know that love is not relative; it is absolute. Love is something that we should keep on giving, no matter what we are faced with. It is not a true form of love if we change our minds about giving as our circumstances change. It is not true love that gives based on preferences. It is important to have this attitude of continuous giving; we should keep giving to others even when we face challenges ourselves. Where is the meaning in saying kind words only when we are healthy and not when we are ill? Love should never be ruled by our changing situations.

Love is easy to give when we are happy and blessed with fortunate circumstances. It is easy to show sympathy to others when we know that we are exceptional. It is easy to offer consolation when we believe that we are superior. It is easy to provide comfort to the poor when we live in luxury. When we are living lavishly, it is not difficult to act charitably and offer good will. When we are happy, healthy, and blessed with fortunate circumstances, it takes little effort to encourage those who are miserable, suffering an illness, or living in unfortunate conditions.

What matters is what we do when we face bad times. We should never take our present circumstances for granted, because everyone goes through both good times and bad times. What will you do if you ever become poor? In times of suffering, how much love will you give back to God? And financial poverty is not the only type of poverty that exists in our world. Many of us will also suffer from spiritual poverty—for example, when our minds become battered by failure and setbacks. What will you choose to do in tough times like these? It is not difficult to take care of the sick when we are healthy, but how much care and attention will you be able to give when you become ill yourself? How thoughtful will you be to the sick when you do not feel well? And how much care will you be able to offer those who are happy if you are feeling miserable?

All of us will be tested on how much love we can share during times of adversity. For example, which do you think means more to God: a penniless man's donation of one candle or a millionaire's offering of ten thousand or even a hundred million candles? I believe that God feels greater joy from larger sacrifices than from smaller ones. Those of you who possess wealth should aim to make large contributions to society, and those of you who live by meager means should give what you can. There was a time when churches collected tithes and both the wealthy and the poor donated one-tenth of their income to God. This encouraged all Christians to practice repaying God for the blessings God had provided. I believe that this is a good metaphor for a basic spirit of love.

Life is a succession of waves, both large and small. Whether we are riding out a gentle wave or desperately trying to maintain our balance during a treacherous surge, we should keep on giving. It is not difficult to smile when we receive a sincere complement. But it's difficult to keep smiling when someone treats us with hostility. Despite this, it is our duty to make the effort to keep on smiling. No matter what we face, we should never stop loving. We should never abandon love. In the final analysis, continuity is a fundamental element of love. It is an essential part of loving to keep on giving. Love is the safety rope around our friend's waist. Just as mountain climbers never lose their grip on each other's rope, we must never lose our grip on love.

Where is the merit in loving those who love us back? Even dogs and deer are capable of loving their parents, who take care of them. And dogs and deer will love their children for looking up to them. Even animals have no difficulty giving love to those who love them. But people can choose a higher perspective. For the sake of our own spiritual discipline, we should aim to give love to the people that most others will not choose to love.

Some of the people we know will make mistakes and abandon the path to God's Truths. We should never judge and label these people as sinners for making that mistake. We should never believe that they deserve to lose their way. For true love never forsakes anyone. As I said long ago, it is the shepherd's duty to find his lost sheep in the valley, even if it means taking the risk of leaving behind his herd of ninety-nine other sheep. This is the way God loves us. God's love never deserts anyone, and neither shall ours.

God's love is like a father's or mother's love for a child. Fathers and mothers don't stop loving their children just because they behave badly, and they do not start loving them again just because they behave well. In fact, the worse a child behaves, the more the child's parents worry, provide care and attention, and offer help and support to the child. They do this because they cherish their children.

This is how God feels about all people. Everyone is a child of God. And because everyone is a child of God, we should cherish everyone who obeys God. But it is those who do not follow God who require more of our care and attention. It is easy to love the pure and innocent, but we must also love those who have become lost and have made mistakes.

LOVE BRINGS US TOGETHER IN ALL OUR IMPERFECTIONS

The goal of love is to join everyone's hands together and never let go. Love is about tying a safety rope to each and every person, helping everyone band together, and keeping on going. We should never sever anyone's climbing rope for the sake of saving ourselves. The goal of love is to carry each and every soul to the mountaintop, no matter how painful and difficult the climb becomes. We will keep on climbing and keep on supporting one another. This is the essence and the goal of love.

Love never abandons anyone. Love never stops trying to help everyone grow and hold hands with others. A loving person never ostracizes others or creates an exclusive circle of friends. What is the purpose of creating harmony among your friends? Instead, we should aspire to unite all different kinds of people.

A loving person never wants to be the only one who is happy. Love means always praying for greater happiness for everyone. Love means knowing that you and I are part of the same whole. You and I are not strangers but parts of each other. This understanding is the foundation of love.

If we have enemies, it is often the case that they just have not realized that we are all brothers and sisters. And no matter how much effort we make to help them realize this truth, it may never be easy for them to accept it. But this should not change the way we love them. It is not true love to criticize the people who think they are your enemies, expose their ignorance, and try to prove their inferiority. True love waits patiently for others to awaken to the Truths. This is the overwhelming love that we should aspire to live by. So don't ever give in to anger or discouragement if someone pushes you away when you offer a helping hand. Just remember that the person you are trying to help does not yet know that you are a brother or sister—a friend who has come to help.

Real love has no enemies, because love means always praying for each and every person's growth. If we see someone as an enemy, we should check to figure out if our love is weak. If we ever make anyone angry, we should check to figure out if our words were hurtful or poisonous, or whether somewhere within us, we wished for their unhappiness. If we discover any of these mistakes in ourselves, we should pray for God's forgiveness.

It is difficult to criticize anyone who possesses overwhelming goodness. It is impossible for people to speak negatively about someone who always tries to help them regardless of the circumstances. On the other hand, people do tend to criticize those who criticize them. Demons can only be summoned by demons. If a strong evil appears as your enemy, then you must take that as a sign that there was an equally strong evil within you that summoned that enemy. It is not only our enemies who should practice self-reflection; we should too.

Telling people facts about themselves is not always righteous when it is intended as a criticism. Instead, we should make the effort to nurture others with as little pain as possible. If someone you

trust were to criticize you, would you be able to respond with gratitude? You might have the strength to thank them, but deep inside,
the hurt and frustration you would feel would probably be stronger
than your gratitude. The more you respect that person, the deeper
your hurt would be. So why not aspire to be a friend who never
criticizes? Why not try to be a friend who never speaks negatively
about anyone? This could be the right way to live our lives.

No one is perfect. If we criticize our peers for their weaknesses
and they criticize us for our imperfections, where will we find love?
We will never be able to create an ideal world. So when someone
criticizes us, that is the perfect time to think about that person's
good qualities. It could be a wonderful chance to discover something beautiful within that person.

LOVE AND FORGIVENESS

Close your eyes, calm your mind, and ask yourself how many people
you have forgiven over the course of your life. Most of you will probably have forgiven fewer than ten people. Now close your eyes again,
and ask yourself how many people you have hurt over the course of
your life. How many people have you caused emotional or financial
turmoil? Most people will probably count far more than ten.

Compare the number of people you have hurt and the number
of people you have forgiven in your life so far, and ask yourself
whether you can say with good conscience that you have been a
good person. If you have hurt fewer than ten people, perhaps it is
fair to say that you do not have to forgive more than ten people.
But most of you will probably realize that you have never forgiven
anyone before, but have hurt many. Many of you will also notice
that this is the first time you realized this. This is the way that the
majority of us are going through life.

It is human nature to exaggerate other people's imperfections while minimizing our own shortcomings. We have a hard time forgiving people for their mistakes but find it easy to forgive ourselves for the same things. We must realize that we have imperfections and everyone else does too.

Remember a situation when a friend had offended you but did not realize it. You probably judged your friend for being insensitive, but the truth is that you have probably made the same mistake at some point in your life. Every one of us should quietly reflect upon the decades we have lived so far and think about how many people's feelings we may have hurt. Did you ever betray the trust and confidence of those who cared about you: your father, mother, brothers, sisters, friends, teachers, and colleagues? Try to remember all the times when you hurt your friends and family members. You will probably remember countless instances and realize how sinfully you have been living.

Now that you have remembered these moments, you can aim to forgive more people than you have hurt. You can apologize to the people you have hurt, and if you cannot apologize to them in person, you can ask for their forgiveness in your heart. If asking them for forgiveness does not seem to work, then turn to God and ask for God's forgiveness. God will surely forgive you for your errors.

There is no one who has never committed any sins. There is no one who has never hurt another person. Long ago, I said, "Let anyone among you who is without sin be the first to throw a stone at her" (John 8:7). Only those of you who have never hurt anyone have the right to call someone else a sinner. Only those of you who have never felt evil in your heart have the right to call someone else evil. Only those of you who have never done anything shameful should shame others for their actions. We do not have the right to criticize others.

The root of our ability to forgive is clear self-knowledge. Deep and thorough reflection on our actions allows all of us to realize that we have no right to criticize others. And when we practice forgiveness, we forgive not only others but also ourselves. When we forgive others, we are also forgiving ourselves and asking God to pardon us.

How many people do you think have succeeded at forgiving more than one hundred people? There are very few who have ever had such strength. Now, imagine how many people God has forgiven. If the world's population is five billion, then God has forgiven all five billion of us. We can see that God's mind is vastly superior to any of our minds. No matter how exceptional we may think we are, none of us has ever been able to match God's forgiveness.

God wants to save everyone. God sends many of His children to Earth to help guide the world to salvation. But despite all the effort God makes to save people, many people misunderstand God's love. No matter how patiently God waits for them to take hold of the lifeline He offers, they continue to misunderstand Him and suspect Him of trying to rob them of their freedom. They misunderstand Him as trying to make them victims of restriction and control. We need to stand by the people who misunderstand God; we need to believe that they will awaken someday. We should never judge them for falling prey to the influences of evil spirits. We must continue to pray for them, no matter what happens to them.

"Love your enemies, and pray for those who persecute you" (Matt. 5:44) is a pearl of wisdom that we should live by. More precisely, we should love those who *seem* to be our enemies and pray for those who *seem* to persecute us. Enemies do not really exist; enemies are only suffering from a misunderstanding.

So keep giving love, and keep praying from your heart for those who persecute you, for I guarantee that your sincerity will reach them someday. Wait patiently for them to change. It is not about give-and-take. Never expect anything in return. Be like God, who gives without limit. It is our duty to give and keep giving.

THE SOURCE OF LOVE

What is the source of love? Why is it important for us to contemplate love? Why did I spend my life teaching about love? Because the goal of our lives is to find out who we are. On our journey through life we search for love, too, and eventually discover the love within us. We discover that love is the goal of our lives.

Love is the goal of our lives because love is God. And if God is love, we also betray ourselves when our actions transgress love. We need to be honest with ourselves and awaken to the love inside us. Even if no one responds to the love we give, we should never become angry, complain, or feel resentful. Instead, we should take it as a sign that we need to make our love much bigger.

The love within us is like a spring that never stops flowing, no matter how much water we take from it. Love does not count how many people's thirst it has quenched. Look within yourself and envision the love inside you flowing like a spring. Make the spring within you an infinite fountain that will never stop supplying water.

Since ancient times, springs have supplied valuable water to travelers. Even hot desert lands have always had oases that provided water. These oases have never charged a penny for their water, and they have never stopped giving. We should be like these oases. As long as we keep digging a deep oasis, a deep well, a deep spring within our hearts, our love will never run dry, no matter how many people come to drink our water from it.

We should never tell anyone that they cannot drink from our well. Instead, we must dig deeper so we can make our well large enough to quench their thirst. We should keep digging our well deeper throughout our lives so we can be like the spring that keeps pouring forth water out of its own abundance.

Love is the life of God, and the life of God is a clear spring that never stops flowing, no matter how much we draw from it. God is the source of our love, and the love of God is like a vast, never-ending well. When we dig our own well deeper, we ultimately discover an enormous channel of water running deep underground that is connected to a vast web of other underground channels of water.

It is up to each of us to keep digging until we reach these channels. The underground stream may be thirty meters deep, but many of us will stop at twenty-nine meters, not knowing that the underground river lies just one meter deeper. Many of us will also stop at five meters because we are satisfied by the small spring of water we find at the shallow levels. But if you keep on digging, as far as you can, you eventually hit that deepest vein of spring water, and you experience God's tremendous spirit. At that deepest level, you will feel God's limitless energy and power.

Therefore, we should regret how little love we have within us, how shallow we have dug our well. If our well were so deep that it was always overflowing with love, then there could be no conflict, no matter how many people came to use it. It is only because our well is not deep enough that we have not been able to quench everyone's thirst.

THE RESURRECTION OF LOVE

This spiritual message I am giving you breaks my two thousand years of silence. In those two thousand years, I have been providing guidance to religious leaders as I kept watch from Heaven. But never in all of history have I spoken directly to someone living on Earth. I hope that people on Earth today will understand the importance of this resurrection and rejoice in this miracle.

I know that you will face strong skepticism. Ironically, Christians will be the first to be skeptical of my resurrection. But regardless of whether they believe my message or not, my message to all Christians and all non-Christians is the same: God has not abandoned you. God will never desert you. God will never make orphans of you.

Please know that God's hands are always at work somewhere in this world and His tremendous power is always operating around us. God's love has directly and indirectly cast its sunshine upon this world in many different ways through the ages. He has sent many men and women to Earth to spread His teachings, spread the fine arts, propagate literature, and disseminate philosophy. All of these have been forms of God's breath breathing life into the world. If you believe that God has breathed his miracles upon us in the past, then believe that he is continuing to do so today.

I often hear that many people today do not believe in the existence of spirits and the spirit world. Even religious people who believe in the existence of the spirit world may not believe that many great figures from Heaven are capable of giving spiritual messages to people on Earth.

So my question to you all is this: which will you choose? Will you choose to bet your hopes on God's salvation? Or will you choose to live without hope of salvation? If you do not need the hope of God's salvation, then you should go on your way. But if you do need God's salvation, you must change your attitude. Throughout history, in every age, God has created miracles. He has extended His hand of salvation in every era. Therefore, you must believe that His hand is still at work in the present. There is a reason I am speaking to you right now through this spiritual message, and it is important for as many people as possible to understand that reason.

It is your choice to believe or not to believe, but the difference between believing and disbelieving is the difference between living with and without profound peace of mind. Which do you think will give you more happiness: to believe that God is extending his hand of salvation to you right now, or to deny Him? What good will it do to deny God's help? Is there anything to gain from denying Him? To deny God's hand is to deny God's help along the path toward Him and to deny His protection from the temptations of materialism. Do not disbelieve everything just because you can find reason for doubt. Take a look at everything one more time with a fresh eye, and search for the Truth that you may have missed before.

Did you really believe that I would not be resurrected in this age of turmoil and crisis? I am with you again in this moment, because I cherish and love you all so very dearly. I am with you now not as a physical being, but as life, as words, as this resounding voice. I am resurrected as love—and this message is the resurrection of my love. I come to you now not as a weak human being, but as a profound source of life that will never dry out, no matter how much I give. I have come as a spring of love, a spring of words. As you believe in this resurrection, so you will receive tremendous courage. You will know with confidence that you are living in an age of glory.

And just as I am giving this spiritual message to my followers on Earth, other spirits will also be providing spiritual messages to their followers. And just as Christians may not believe that this message comes from me, the followers of other religions may also be skeptical of the spiritual messages that their founders send.

But if we think about God's nature and what God would do, we will realize that God would never keep his silence forever. God will always find ways to help His people. So you must consider whether these spiritual messages may be the work of God's hands, manifestations of God's love reaching out to you.

Jesus Christ was not a weak man who died on a cross two thousand years ago. No, Jesus Christ continues to exist today and has been working tirelessly throughout those two thousand years to provide guidance to people from his residence in Heaven. I have not rested a single day as I have sought to fulfill my mission. I have never stopped working; I have never rested. I have worked night and day to make your lives happier and fill them with more love. Please know and believe that I have been guiding you to help you find deeper faith.

Right now, I reside in the ninth dimension and have taken the reins to begin the movement of spreading the Truths. There is a reason I have taken the reins: I am in charge of purifying Earth and providing salvation. I am the guiding spirit who has been entrusted with this responsibility. My resurrection will mark the beginning of a great movement of salvation. Do not misunderstand the purpose of this great movement. Do not become preoccupied in ostracizing or criticizing people of different religions. Simply believe in the power of God's profound salvation. Do not allow your foolish pride and ego to cloud your judgment. Believe that Jesus Christ will not keep silent in this age of chaos.

Many of my sheep have incarnated on Earth to help build the new age to come. My sheep will find their way back to me. So my beloved sheep, when you hear my voice, seek me out and find your way straight to me. The more you seek, the more I shall give. Seek more from me, because I am here to keep supplying you with my love. Seek my love as an infant seeks his mother's milk. Seek from me the power of life. Do not seek it from others. Only seek it from me.

My beloved sheep, return to me. I shall praise you, cherish you, heal you of your fatigue, and love you from my heart. I shall forgive you and I shall embrace you. Return to me, your shepherd, for the sun has begun to set. When the sun begins to set, listen for the shepherd's call, his horn, and his bell and find your way back to me. You shall remember my familiar voice. Follow that voice and return to me, for I shall take you to the mountain summit. Bring my people to me. Return the sheep to their shepherd, for their shepherd has returned to them.

II. My Mission of Faith

HUMILITY

The will of my Heavenly Father is so profound that it has often defied my understanding. When I was on Earth, His will was far beyond my comprehension. I knew that I was one of His servants and that He had entrusted me with a mission, but I could not see the full extent of my role. From a worldly perspective, the majority of His messages would have been seen as completely unreasonable, but it was not my place to ask Him why things had to be that way. This is why Christians developed a value for the virtue of obedience.

God demands obedience not because he wants to create a military-like order, but because His mind is beyond human description. When we live in physical bodies, our awareness becomes restricted to our physical bodies, so many of us, even those who originally come from a high place in Heaven, become vulnerable to skepticism about the simplest of matters.

Obedience is very valuable, especially for believers, because God's intentions are so profound that they are virtually impossible to believe and understand, no matter how thoroughly we explain them. It could take two thousand years to fully understand the purpose behind some of his commands. We would be very fortunate if we could figure out God's intentions within decades or even centuries. I would have been infinitely grateful if I could have clearly comprehended the intentions behind my mission while I was still alive. But this would have also meant that my mission was small and relatively easy.

This is why we should not judge between good and evil or true and false based on how well or how easily we can comprehend something. It is extraordinarily challenging to maintain a spiritual perspective all the time. To remind us to think from a spiritual point of view, God always provides us with trials that test us for overreliance on worldly values. God's paradoxes, like many Zen koans, are some of the ways He teaches us to aim beyond worldly successes and reach beyond the easy path through life.

THE HEAVENLY FATHER

The doctrine of the Holy Trinity was developed by theologians who did not understand the spirit world and could not tell the difference between God and His servants. They perceived all the divine spirits, including God, as the same. Since it has not been important for the majority of people to know the details of Heaven's secrets, they have only very rarely been revealed. So we should not trust the debates of professional theologians who do not possess spiritual abilities. Since they have never seen the Holy Trinity with their own eyes, their theories are simply ideas that they formed in their heads.

But this much is true: as the Bible clearly describes me saying, my Heavenly Father sent me to Earth. I was the first person in history to call God "my Heavenly Father," and Christianity is known today for being the first religion to introduce the belief that God is our Father who resides in Heaven. And since the Father in Heaven

45

was the one and only God in the Christian world, my calling Him "Father in Heaven" meant that I sat at the right hand of God.

As you may know, long before my time, the Hebrew Bible was already teaching that hosts of angels are helping the people who live in this world. As you can tell from paintings of angels depicted with halos and wings, Christians continued this belief. However, the number of angels that actually exists is vastly greater than what my believers ever imagined, and the size of the world of angels is so great that it is far beyond human comprehension. The truth is that there has been and always will be many active angels outside the world of Christianity. Christians used halos in their paintings to indicate that the figures in the paintings were angels, and they used wings to symbolize the fact that angels help souls on Earth and in Hell "fly"—that is, rise up—to Heaven. But these symbols are only meant to facilitate people's understanding and show that divine beings exist—they are not meant to be taken literally. This is why Buddhist depictions of angels do not use these same motifs.

It is not important for most people to understand the deep relationship between the Heavenly Father and me or the positions held by the Holy Spirit, the angels, and me. I am just one of many of the Heavenly Father's keys that help people open the gates of Heaven. The Heavenly Father has many ways to guide people; He holds many keys to Heaven in His hands and has entrusted many angels to hold additional keys.

Through His angels, God has created many different religions, and I believe that it is arrogant for the Christian church to preach that there is no other way into Heaven except through Christ. Christianity is not the only religion with active angels. It is more valuable for everyone to know that many divine beings equivalent to Christian angels are serving the many religions that God has established.

Still, I am sure that you would like to know more about the being that I call my Heavenly Father and how I experienced Him through my life. While I was alive, I was able to see the spiritual forms of past prophets such as Moses and Elijah, but even I was not able to see the image of my Heavenly Father nor fully comprehend who He was. I was only able to hear His voice. So you can imagine that it is very difficult for those of you in this world to gain a clear grasp of who our Heavenly Father is. Even I was only permitted to hear His voice.

I would describe our Heavenly Father as Truth. Truth is His other name. The hands of Truth are always at work upon the living creatures of this world; nevertheless, we can only ever catch a glimpse of this Truth through symbols and other indirect means. It is extremely difficult for us to directly experience our Heavenly Father—to see, hear, and understand Him. But we can experience Him through Truth.

Now I am in Heaven, but it is still very difficult to give a thorough description of God in worldly, human, or symbolic terms. But I would like everyone to know that from my perspective in Heaven, my impression of the Heavenly Father is close to the image of the Hindu god who is depicted with multiple arms. The numerous arms represent God's salvation. He needs many arms to save the people of many different countries and many different races, and I am just one of those arms. Though these arms know that they are a part of God's body, they can never see the full form of the body that they are attached to. Therefore, what I can tell you is this: God is Truth, and Truth can change Itself into many forms to lead countless souls to salvation.

GRATITUDE TO GOD

God seeks neither gratitude nor glorification. It is the clergy's idea that people must praise and thank God. But this world is an imperfect world, full of miserable people, and many of these people will lose hope if we insist that this is the only truth of this world. By teaching people about a perfect world and the existence of perfect happiness, we can help them find the strength to persist through suffering and adversity. It is because people need the strength to keep going in difficult times that we revere God as a perfect being.

In the final analysis, gratitude and glory are not what God seeks from us. God is devoted to finding ways to help people endure through difficulties. God wants us to teach people about the world that is waiting for them in the afterlife.

So is there any virtue in praising and thanking God? It depends on the level of self-awareness that grounds our praise and gratitude. Our faith is very immature if we give gratitude and glory to God to try to get God to pardon our sins. If we have committed wrongs, then we must harvest the fruits of those seeds while we are alive. We must self-reflect, repent, and return what we have borrowed. We may ask God to forgive our weaknesses and to give us strength. But we must remember that if giving God gratitude and glorification had the power to negate or hide our sins, then Hell would have disappeared long ago.

FAITH AND MIRACLES

Faith is a necessary condition in creating miracles, because all living creatures have a contract with God. The Creator is free to decide whether to preserve or let go of anything in this world, and He is free to decide whether or not to heal an illness. But we could fall into the clutches of the Devil if we were to misunderstand this contract as a way to hold God responsible for everything that happens. It is dangerous to think of our contract with God the way we think of business contracts.

Some Christian sects teach that your thoughts have the power to create material reality. There is truth in this teaching, but it is also true that many of our wishes do not come true. There are times when faith in God will produce miracles, but God does not create miracles in exchange for faith the way a business associate fulfills the terms of a worldly contract.

God does not always give us what we wish for, because the purpose of this world is to be a place where our souls can learn and grow. If we allow our faith to depend only on God's salvation, we risk falling into the trap of believing that God is responsible for everything. It is not God, but we who should take responsibility for the seeds that we sowed in the past. It is up to us to harvest the fruits that are born from our seeds; miracles will not harvest them for us or produce a different harvest. As we often say, we must reap what we sow.

Sometimes, miracles defy this spiritual law and make unforesee-able things happen. But even when such cases occur, unfortunately, many of today's Christians are so skeptical that they cannot believe in the miracles that are occurring around them. Even if Saint Mary miraculously heals the sick at the spring of Lourdes, hospitals ada-mantly refuse to provide written confirmation that those illnesses have been healed. I cannot hold back my tears of shock when I see such strong effects of materialism.

But when many people's minds run to one extreme, self-reflection eventually sets in. An age based on spirituality will eventually arrive as self-reflection opens more and more people up to a spiritual way of life. Many of you have survived a century of materialism and war, but now, a completely different era is beginning.

MY MISSION ON EARTH

Original Sin

The concept that we are children of sin existed in Judaism before my time. The idea of original sin comes from the Book of Genesis in the Hebrew Bible. The Book of Genesis describes God creating Heaven and Earth and separating one from the other. Then, mankind, animals, and plants were brought into creation. In the Garden of Eden, though, Eve gained the knowledge of good and evil when she ate from the Tree of Knowledge. To punish Adam and Eve for disobeying Him, God gave them suffering, work, and the pain of childbirth.

Then, one thousand years before my birth, a prophet foretold that a Messiah would be sent to Earth. The prophet said that the Messiah would be slain and ascend into Heaven. It may be true that my birth fulfilled this prophecy, but I was not born to atone for the sins of humankind.

The truth is that the concept of original sin developed over the course of Christian history. It was not my goal to die on the cross to atone for humankind's sins. God gave me my mission and commanded me to enter Jerusalem, and prophecies foretold that it was my destiny to die there. I knew that I had to accept my fate as God commanded. Still, my heart was deeply grieved that I had to die and leave this world before more people had the chance to believe in my teachings. When I was carrying the cross up the hill, and while I was being hung onto the cross, my heart was filled with regret that I had to leave much of my mission unfinished. But I entrusted myself to God's will and abided by the inspirations I received. I was simply following God's commands.

The Jews and the Roman soldiers tried and convicted me, and I was crucified in Golgotha between other criminals. That was how the life of Jesus in the flesh ended. You probably know from the Bible about the countless miracles I performed. So as I faced my death, even I could not understand why such a human death was ordained to me, and even I could not comprehend the meaning that my death held. I healed many people and spread the gospel to countless people through my ministry. But instead of believing in me, the majority of the people sided with the men who tried and convicted me. Even my disciples left me. My religious order was destroyed as I faced my death, and I wondered myself whether God's design would truly succeed.

It was never my intention to die on the cross to atone for everyone's sins. After my death, however, the cross became a symbol of Christianity. It contributed to the spread of the Christian faith, and through missionary work, this faith helped save many people. The doctrine of original sin did not come from me, but was created by my disciples, who sought to spread the word that Jesus did not die in vain.

Today, two thousand years after my death, there are as many as two billion Christians on Earth. Two billion people have found faith as a result of this single grain of wheat that sacrificed its life. It would have been impossible to spread the Christian faith to two billion people during my lifetime. The world population probably had not even reached two billion yet. I reflect with awe at how widely this single grain of wheat has spread.

The Meaning of the Cross

It has probably been excruciating for Christians to worship the image of me on a cross wearing a crown of thorns, because this image represents the blood I spilled. It is painful to believe that God's only son, who is your Lord, died on the cross wearing a crown of thorns, with blood streaming down his face, his legs broken, and nails hammered into his body. Anyone who sees this image would wonder why someone who believed in God's words met such a tragic end. If I had not believed in God's words, my life would have had a different ending. But I chose to believe, and as a result, I faced a cruel death.

Those who see the image of my crucifixion should realize how weak their faith is in comparison; they should be inspired to repent and deepen their humility. They will realize, as they contemplate this image, that even though God is the Father of our souls, and even though our souls, as God's creations, are precious, we are still no more important than a grain of wheat. Some philosophies teach that we can become gods, but we should not misinterpret these teachings. It is true that some people are very close to God and may some day reach a godly status, but this is not the case for the majority of people.

The message of my crucifixion is that the sacrifice of a single grain of wheat can lead billions of people to salvation. It was also my way of asking whether you can love God as passionately as I loved God. It is very sad that nowadays, the cross has become an empty symbol that only represents a historical event.

It is difficult for people to be strong. It is difficult to have a strong heart. We easily fall prey to temptations of profit and pleasure. We lose sight of the most important things and sell them off for money. You must realize that these temptations could be sneaking into your heart, too. Remember as often as possible that my image on the cross is meant to remind you that you should not seek only worldly victory, worldly gain, or worldly fame, for the man whom God loved the most died a most cruel and tragic death.

Worldly perfection and worldly happiness are not God's goals for you. On the contrary, as you go through life, you will experience countless mistakes and failures, many hardships, and much adversity. Though some illnesses may miraculously heal, many more will not. If you find yourself disappointed and hopeless each time you face one of life's trials, then you should look upon the cross to remind yourself of the virtues of strength and patience. What God hopes for you is that you will live a life of purity that will serve as a model for the generations who come after you.

God sends people to Earth with different roles. Some of us are born to become political and military leaders with a mission to achieve victory in this world, while some of us, are, as I was, born to be a teacher of souls. There are military heroes who incarnate with the mission of actualizing God's glory on Earth. They are entrusted with the job of developing a strong defense against the enemy and valiantly protecting the nation on God's behalf. But this is not a role that people like me are born with. I was born to teach everyone about the truth of our souls and the ways to purify our souls so everyone can live a more meaningful life.

I was a harbinger who was entrusted with the job of signaling the arrival of the Kingdom of God. I was nothing more than a single trumpet that kept on playing, and my work never accomplished anything beyond that.

AUTHOR'S THOUGHTS

JESUS OF THE FLESH, JESUS OF THE SPIRIT

The world is full of all kinds of temptations, delusions, and worldly forms of bondage that drag people down. One result is that people tend to believe only in what they can see with their own eyes. I believe that there is a difference between the Jesus Christ that his disciples believed in during his ministry and the Jesus Christ that people believe in today, two thousand years later.

The Jesus Christ that his disciples saw during his ministry was a man who suffered the same persecutions that they suffered, who had difficulty finding food and shelter, and who was betrayed, stoned by the masses, dragged behind by Roman soldiers, and crucified between two thieves. Jesus's disciples and contemporaries saw his human side, and his humanity caused many people to doubt him.

Non-Christians often criticize Christians for believing in a man who could not even save his own life. Those who sneered at and tormented Jesus during his crucifixion followed the same logic. They ridiculed him, writing on a placard, "Long live the King of the Jews," and placed a crown of thorns on his head. They jeered at and taunted him, daring him to prove to them that he was the King of the Jews and the Messiah. But a miracle never occurred, and Jesus never escaped from the cross.

But people of later generations saw a different Jesus. Instead of the human Jesus, they believed in the resurrected Jesus, the only Son of God. In time, many people began to believe in Jesus and God as one being. The Jesus that people of later generations came to believe in is closer to the true Jesus.

After his crucifixion, Jesus was spiritually resurrected, and his resurrection taught us that our souls have eternal life. When he showed himself to his disciples, he told them about the other world and taught them that the soul is imperishable and eternal.

JESUS AND GOD

Till the end of his life, Jesus always knew that there was a God, his Father, and that he was His son. He often said, "Whoever has seen me has seen the Father" (John 14:9). It is clear that Jesus was aware of a spiritual Father; he often prayed to Him, and he distinguished himself from his Father. Some parts of the Bible show the spirit of the Father talking through Jesus, but people of later generations misunderstood this and began to confuse the Father in Heaven with Christ the son, believing that both were God.

Jesus often called out, "My Lord, my Lord!" As I explained in my book, *The Laws of the Sun*, he was calling El Cantare. The God that Jesus believed in was the God of love, El Cantare—not the god of ancient Israel. El Cantare was his Lord. This fact is the key that untangles the complicated aspects of Christianity and solves the mystery of Jesus's crucifixion. It is obvious from Jesus's teachings that he believed in the God of love. The God of love who was guiding Jesus from Heaven was El Cantare.

By contrast, the god of ancient Israel was a god of contracts. Yahweh promised to protect those who obeyed him and threatened to punish those who did not. In the Hebrew Bible, Yahweh appears whenever there are floods, illnesses, and wars—in short, when humankind is suffering punishment. In ancient Israel, Yahweh was the god of mountains and curses.

Yahweh and the God of love are completely different beings, but Jesus was not aware of this during his ministry on Earth. He had only three years to administer his teachings, and that was not enough time to organize his spiritual knowledge. Jesus had the ability to receive revelations from many spirits. However, he understood all of them as the voice of God. He did not realize that many divine spirits with different personalities and varying opinions were speaking to him. He did not know that listening to one spirit brings about a completely different outcome from listening to a different spirit. He was not able to see through this confusion.

THE STRUGGLE BETWEEN YAHWEH AND EL CANTARE: TRADITIONAL JUDAISM OR A WORLDWIDE RELIGION OF LOVE?

Jesus considered himself one of the Jewish prophets and a rabbi. He was versed in the laws of the Torah that had been written after Moses's time, and he had been giving talks about civil laws.

The Torah scholars of Jesus's time were conservatives who adhered strictly to formalism of law. Many of them accused Jesus of teaching his own original philosophy and violating the traditional doctrines of Judaism. For example, the Torah prohibits people from working on the Sabbath, but Jesus healed the ill on the Sabbath. Since Jesus believed in the God of love, he never hesitated to help people whenever he was needed. The scholars accused him of violating the laws of the Torah, but Jesus chose to prioritize his love of those who were suffering over the laws. This became one of the reasons for his persecution: his behavior spurred conflict between those who adhered to traditional forms and rules and those who believed that God's will is not found in following rules but in practicing acts of love.

During his ministry, Jesus often referred to the Hebrew Bible to explain his way of thinking and acting. He would quote a teaching and try to explain how to put that teaching into practice. In the eyes of the conservative Jews who followed traditional interpretations of the Torah, Jesus appeared to be preaching wrong interpretations. The conservative Jews also came to fear that if Jesus's teachings continued to spread like wildfire throughout the lands, all the traditional teachings of Judaism, as passed down from Moses, would completely disappear. This was the beginning of Jesus's persecution.

In addition, Jesus identified as a Jew. He expected to live as a Jew and die as a Jew. Unfortunately, he was unable to identify with non-Jews. For example, one Bible passage shows Jesus saying that his teachings are meant only for Jews and not for Samaritans. But when he is told that Samaritans deserve to at least receive the leftovers of his teachings, Jesus acknowledges that this is true.

In stories like this one, we catch glimpses of Jesus trying but also struggling to grow beyond the confines of the Jewish community. That this was a struggle for him testifies to the limitations of his culture at that time; it also shows how being confined to a corporeal body limited his awareness. El Cantare told him that his teachings would create a new world religion and encouraged him to work beyond the boundaries of the Jewish community and sow the seeds of love as widely as he could. On the other hand, spirits related to Yahweh wanted to confine him to the lineage of Jewish prophets.

Unfortunately, Jesus could not differentiate between the voice of the God who commanded him to build a new world religion and the voices that coaxed him to return to the teachings of Moses and revive the traditional teachings of Judaism. In the final analysis, Jesus was crucified by the forces that wanted to confine his stature to that of a Jewish prophet.

After Jesus died and was resurrected, the apostle Paul experienced an awakening and began spreading Jesus's teachings. As El Cantare had planned, Jesus's teachings eventually spread throughout the world and became a worldwide, universal religion. Ultimately, over the course of time, El Cantare's designs triumphed.

CHAPTER 2

SHAKYAMUNI BUDDHA

The Path to Enlightenment

THE LIFE OF SHAKYAMUNI BUDDHA

HIS EARLY LIFE AND DISCOVERY OF THE MIDDLE WAY

Gautama Siddhartha was born as the prince and expected king of the Shakya clan, which had built and ruled a country that extended across parts of modern-day North India and Nepal. His mother, Maya, died from puerperal fever just one week after giving birth to Gautama. His father, King Suddhodana, then married his wife's sister, Prajapati, an extremely virtuous woman who raised Gautama with loving care.

As Gautama grew up, he lived a life of material comfort, with separate palaces for summer, winter, and the monsoon season, and he had a different wife in each of these palaces. But after living this way for a while, he became aware of the contradictions and the impermanence of life. Spiritual questions welled up within him, and at the age of twenty-nine, he decided to set off in search of the answers to his questions. He left his home, the Kapilavastu palace, just after his wife Yashodhara gave birth to Rahula, his only son.

Gautama gave up all the things of this world, including his family and his status as a prince, to seek a mentor who could answer his questions about life. In spite of his efforts, he never found the right teacher. Instead, he spent the next six years seeking enlightenment by following an ascetic lifestyle in the company of five other spiritual seekers. Of the six, Gautama was the most enthusiastic about asceticism and won the praise of the others for his commitment to it. He tried living on a single grain of millet each day. He tried burying his body, leaving only his head above ground so that he could breathe, and he tried meditating seated on a craggy cliff. As a result of his ascetic training, he was reduced to skin and bone.

One day, he went to the Nairanjana River to bathe, but his body was so light that he began to float away in the water. He had become so thin that he was carried away like a piece of driftwood, unable even to stand up in the water. This experience made him wonder if it was right to go on living the way he had been. Asceticism and self-mortification had made him so weak and faint that he thought he would soon die if he continued this way. At that moment, a village girl named Sujata passed by and offered him a bowl of milk porridge. Gautama accepted the bowl of porridge. The moment he sipped it, he felt his body fill with energy, and he had an epiphany:

"For years, I have tormented my body in pursuit of enlightenment. But if this kind of self-mortification were the true purpose and mission of life on Earth, wouldn't it mean that it is a mistake to be born into this world in the first place? If spiritual refinement means denying life in the physical body, then human beings shouldn't be born into this world.

"But neither was I able to find answers to my questions about the meaning of life at Kapilavastu, where I led a life of luxury, rich in material comfort and pleasure. In a life of indulgence, I found only corruption. That path led only to degeneracy and denied all possibility of improving human nature. I could not possibly have attained true enlightenment in that sort of life, full of pleasure, decadence, and idle wealth. That life just prevented me from refining my character. A life taken up with extremes of affluence and pleasure cannot lead people to true happiness—at least, not to the happiness that is called enlightenment."

This experience led Gautama to the first stage of his enlightenment, which was the discovery of the Middle Way. He realized that, in practicing spiritual discipline, it is essential to keep to the Middle Way between pain and pleasure. He had discovered that the path to enlightenment is found neither in the pain of rigorous asceticism nor in the pleasures of a luxurious life; it is to be found only in rejecting these two extremes. Gautama denied both the asceticism that tormented the body and the Epicureanism that forestalled spiritual growth. He had discovered that he could neither improve his intellect nor find true wisdom by living in either of these extreme ways. With the goal of rebuilding his severely weakened body, he abandoned extreme asceticism and started to accept alms when they were offered, meanwhile continuing his meditation practice to gain deeper insights.

Soon after Gautama decided to accept food offerings, he found peace and harmony in his mind. He realized that practicing asceticism had led him to become feeble in both body and in mind and that it had led him to be overcome by passive and negative thoughts. He had been too concerned about being independent and had refused to accept any help from others in collecting food and getting other necessities. He realized that he had been in a constant state of extreme tension, like strings that had been tightened too much on a lute. He decided to stop putting such undue strain on himself and stop lying to himself, pretending that he did not really have an appetite. He decided to abandon all pretense and practice moderation.

Gautama was surprised, as he became more relaxed about life, how precisely he was able to observe others. He realized he wanted to see people's lives accurately so he could give each person advice that was appropriate for that person's unique situation. He also wanted to be able to assess himself accurately. He wanted to understand the meaning of this world and of human life and actually experience the enlightenment that so many seekers search for. He wanted to know what it really meant to become a buddha—an enlightened one. Gautama felt that he heard a voice saying, "Give up your old life and take a new path." So he set out on a journey, and several days later, he arrived in a town called Gaya.

GIVING UP INNER ATTACHMENT AND ATTAINING
GREAT ENLIGHTENMENT

In Gaya, Gautama took up the life of a mendicant. During the day, he did his rounds gathering alms, and from dusk to dawn he set aside time for his quest for enlightenment. He made it a rule to start meditating at sunset under a big pipal tree not far from the river. The tree provided him with ample shelter—it was so big around that two people could not encircle its trunk with their arms outstretched.

He concentrated mainly on reflective meditation. Simply trying to focus his mind on a single thought with his eyes closed tended to invite the intervention of evil spirits. To achieve harmony of mind, he instead reflected upon the things he had thought and done since he was a small child. If he recalled situations in which he had gone against his conscience, he tried to put them right. However, as he reflected on the years of his late twenties, a particular thought overwhelmed his mind, no matter how hard he tried to clear it. It was the thought of his wife Yashodhara and his son Rahula. Their faces haunted him. He wondered how big his son had grown, how his wife was doing, and whether she was crying over his absence. These thoughts unsettled him badly.

By this time, a window in Gautama's mind had started to open, and he could hear the voices of beings from the spirit world. One day, while he was sitting in meditation under the pipal tree, a voice began speaking to him from within his mind.

"Gautama, I am Brahma, and I am speaking to you. You spent six years in austerities, in search of enlightenment, but look at what you have achieved as a result of your hard work. It seems that you have simply proved that you are an ordinary person. You have neglected the basic requirements of being human, which are to get married, raise a family, and live happily with your wife and children. You have abandoned your family and the happiness you could have derived from it for the sole purpose of sitting in meditation under a pipal tree. Your life is completely meaningless. You are wrong. Return to Kapilavastu at once, and make your wife and child happy. Living happily with them will pave the path to a great enlightenment for you.

"A human being can never experience happiness in the next life without having enjoyed this one to the fullest. Take as much pleasure as you like in this world. Enjoy this world as fully as you wish. The greater your joy, the more pleasure you will experience in your next life. You haven't enjoyed your life enough. Spend more time enjoying your family life. Feast on a more affluent and elegant lifestyle. That is the kind of self-discipline you should practice in this life."

Gautama found some truth in what the spirit who claimed to be Brahma said. It not only was reasonable and convincing, but also touched a soft spot. Gautama was feeling regret for abandoning his family, and he still felt a strong attachment to his father, his stepmother, and the other people who had raised him so lovingly. No matter how much he repented, he could not deny the fact that he had not been a good son, a good husband, or a good father. His mind was swayed, and he wondered whether he really should return home to the Kapilavastu palace and succeed his father to the throne.

However, one of the remarks the self-proclaimed Brahma made caught his attention: the spirit said that the more Gautama enjoyed this world, the more pleasure he would have in his next life.

It sounded plausible, but Gautama felt that something was slightly wrong with this logic—that the spirit was carefully glossing over something important. He realized that his attachment to this world, still deep inside him, was being brought to light, and that the being that called itself Brahma was actually a devil. Gautama said sternly, "You must be a devil. You call yourself Brahma, but you are most definitely not. Admit that you are really a devil that deludes many seekers. You are Mara Papiyas, the devil; you cannot deceive my eyes." The moment Gautama said this, the voice changed to high-pitched laughter, "Ha-ha-ha! Well done, Gautama, you've found out who I am. How advanced you are in your training! Go on with your training, and live a futile life!"

Gautama's confrontation with the devil named Mara Papiyas taught him that any worldly desire could be an invitation to devils. He realized that the devil actually existed within his own mind. It was not that the devil that existed outside of him was deluding him; this devil had only been attracted by his own weakness or obsession. Devils are drawn to the dark thoughts that lie hidden in a person's mind and feed on them. Whenever a devil can catch a person off guard, it will try to manipulate the person and take total control of his or her mind. So Gautama realized that unless he rid himself of his attachments, there was no way that he would be able to attain a calm state of mind. Even natural, humane thoughts about his wife and son or his father and mother, if they persisted and became obsessive attachments, would cause him to suffer. The devil had used that soft spot to make its way into his mind. He realized that getting rid of attachments in the world of the mind was the first step to enlightenment and that it was different from giving up the desire to eat or being satisfied with humble food and clothing.

As Gautama continued his reflective meditation, he came to

a new understanding: "The mind should always be free of attachment, like a mountain stream that flows freely, without restriction. If the mind concentrates on any one thought, whether good or bad, its freedom is lost, and the stagnant spot becomes an easy target for evil. I had better abandon any sense of obligation and instead enter a state of mind that is more free, open, rich, and peaceful."

Gautama continued to reflect on his whole life of nearly thirty-six years. He discarded any negative thoughts that obsessed his mind and, in so doing, became free of attachment. A great sense of peace enveloped him. He felt the warmth of heavenly light flowing into his chest, and it was at that moment that Gautama truly heard the voice of Brahma.

"Gautama, we are glad that you have at last attained enlightenment. We have been watching over you and waiting for you to reach this first level of enlightenment. Without this enlightenment, you could not fulfill your mission in this lifetime. We were so concerned when you became immersed in a life of luxury and worldly pleasure. When you started your austerities, we worried that you might commit suicide or die from malnutrition. Now you have overcome these difficulties, and you are able to hear our voices. We are truly delighted."

Gautama subsequently gained the ability to see through past, present, and future. He penetrated the secrets of the origin of the universe, the birth and history of planet Earth, the rise and fall of civilizations, his own past incarnations, and the future of humanity. When his mind became still and free from attachment, he experienced his spiritual body expanding to become as big as the whole universe, leaving his physical body behind, beneath the pipal tree. This experience distinguishes one who has unlocked the door to the kingdom of the mind, and it is proof that Gautama had fully grasped the perfect freedom of the soul.

Having attained enlightenment and become the person we now know as the Buddha, Gautama was eager to convey what he had understood to as many people as he could, as quickly as possible. He felt that if he kept the experience to himself, his life would be meaningless. He still wanted to continue his inner journey and reach a deeper level of enlightenment himself, but his urge to convey the Truths to others was so powerful that he could not contain his excitement. So, he took a step forward and began to convey the Truths that his enlightenment had taught him. This moment marked the beginning of Shakyamuni Buddha's mission to preach the Laws, and later came to be known as the First Turning of the Dharma Wheel. He continued this work for the next forty-five years, until the day he passed away at the age of eighty.

A MESSAGE FROM SHAKYAMUNI BUDDHA

I. Seeking the Middle Way

My beloved disciples, listen carefully to my words. You must always have a guide for the mind. Your mind may constantly waver from side to side, but you should keep a guide that points to the right direction for your mind, just as a compass needle points toward the North Star. Words of wisdom will serve as this guide for your mind. Encounter as many words of wisdom as you can, and allow them to nourish your life.

My people, you will not find words of wisdom everywhere. You will receive them when you need them, in the form that you need them, as you go through life. Words can be tricky: unless you use them in the right place, at the right time, and with the right people, you cannot make use of their true power.

My beloved disciples, you will hear my words and sermons differently according to the state of your mind and the time of your life that you encounter them. Thus, you must not interpret my words only in your own ways. You must seek the true meaning of my words. I speak these words not only to help you solve your personal problems; I speak these words to benefit a great many people. From these words, choose the ones that will nourish your mind. Search for what touches your heartstrings. Select the ones that come naturally to you and that you believe to be universal—for those are the words of great wisdom.

ALL THAT YOU DO, YOU DO THROUGH DIVINE POWER
My beloved disciples, you are connected to Eternal Life. You are connected to the life force of the Grand Spirit. You are one with the

life of Buddha; you are a part of His very life.* When you believe in Buddha and practice His Laws, you will achieve countless feats and accomplishments. You will witness many mighty miracles.

Do not think that these feats and miracles have come by the virtue of your own power. Do not think that you have accomplished these feats using only your own abilities. These miracles were made possible because you are connected to the life of the great universe. You were able to accomplish these feats because you are one with the Great Wisdom.

My beloved disciples, there is nothing that comes to pass through your power alone. What appears to be accomplished through your own power is, in reality, accomplished through the power of Buddha. You must always keep this humble attitude. You must always keep in mind this secret of the great universe.

Know that you are on the palm of the hand of the Great Buddha. It is because Buddha holds you on His open hand that you are able to walk upon it. When He closes His hand, the universe will plunge into darkness. Only because Buddha opens His hand does the universe continue to exist within infinite light. You must not forget that you are living on His palm.

People are apt to become overconfident in their abilities when their lives are going well. To prevent yourself from becoming conceited, it is vital that you constantly remind yourself of these words of self-admonition. Even if your actions produce wonderful results, do not become overconfident. Do not overestimate your abilities. Do not claim the credit for yourself. Know that all that you do, you do through the power of Buddha.

---

* Editorial note: In this chapter, the term "Buddha" refers to the Creator God. This term should not be confused with "buddha," which refers to anyone who has attained enlightenment, or with "Shakyamuni Buddha," which means "the sage of the Shakya clan" and refers to Gautama Siddhartha.

SUFFERING AND PAIN ARE WHETSTONES FOR YOUR SOUL

My people, you must not grieve in the midst of misery, for it is in times of unhappiness that you become eligible to enter the Middle Way. In these times, you may regret the way you have lived your life. You may dwell on your mistakes, reviewing them one by one. You may feel truly pitiful. In these times of despair, know that you are preparing yourself to enter a golden road.

You must rise again from desperation, for you are the hands and feet of Buddha, a part of His great life. When you become aware of this truth, you will know that there is no such thing as failure in this world. There is no such thing as a setback in this world. You will never find yourself in the depths of misery, for everything that appears to be a failure, setback, or source of unhappiness is given to you as an opportunity to refine your soul. You must learn to think in this way. This perspective lies at the basis of the Laws.

Pain and suffering do not exist for their own sake; they are not allowed to exist all by themselves. Suffering and pain exist only as whetstones for your soul. They are the sandpaper that you can use to refine your soul and make it shine. My people, you must see pain and suffering in this way. Then, when you are in the midst of predicaments, you will realize what destiny is trying to teach you. Learn your lesson, and use it to nourish your soul. Learn from your failures, and return to the Middle Way.

As you walk on this path, you may encounter the same dangers and problems that you encountered in the past. At those times, make use of the knowledge, skills, and wisdom that you have gained from your past experiences. You will not repeat the same mistakes, for the lessons you have learned and the wisdom you have gained will protect you. They will shed light on your mind. Therefore, do not fear failure. Think of failure as a vaccine that Buddha has given you to protect you from even greater future failures. Your failures today will help you achieve greater success tomorrow. Failure is given to you to train your soul and to fill your life with a greater light. When you enter the path of the Middle Way, you will indeed find eternal light.

SUCCESS ON THE MIDDLE WAY IS ACCOMPANIED BY HUMILITY AND GRATITUDE

You may find yourself climbing the ladder of success. But if you do, you must remember that that ladder may simultaneously be leading you toward failure—for the roads to success and failure are opposite sides of the same coin. This truth becomes more evident as the slope becomes steeper.

Those who do not experience success seldom find failure; those who experience many successes experience many failures. Life always has a left and a right, an up and a down, that exist together like intertwined strands of a rope. Thus, you must always remember that happiness and unhappiness are different strands of the same rope. When you shake a rope, you create many peaks and valleys on it. The same rope forms a peak one moment, and a valley the next. The same is true of your life: you will go through many peaks and valleys. No matter where you are in life, make it a rule to be true to your heart, and make it your principle to walk the Middle Way. The philosophy of the Middle Way will lead you to the royal road of life. You can accomplish great success as you walk the Middle Way.

Success achieved on the Middle Way is always accompanied by humility and gratitude; it will create a path that allows all things to prosper in harmony. What does it mean to be humble? It is to remind yourself that you are always receiving the assistance of others as well as from Buddha. By remembering this, you will prevent yourself from becoming conceited. What is gratitude? Gratitude is a state born of humility. You feel grateful only when you are humble. When you have gratitude, you will express your humility in the form of good deeds to others. In times of success, when others are praising you, when you are at the high tide of life, you must discipline yourself to be humble. Stay grateful to others and to Buddha. Your success will continue to grow as long as you remember to be humble and grateful during successful times.

Your successes must not cause others to fail. Your successes must not harm others. Your successes must not bring unhappiness to others. Your path to success must nurture everybody. This path that nurtures everybody is the Middle Way. It is a wide and flat road that continues far into the distance. Know that the Middle Way is also a golden road, for it shines with a golden light. My people, you must understand this truth of the Middle Way.

SUCCESS MEANS BECOMING A CANAL OF LOVE

My beloved disciples, I have always taught you not to pursue happiness only for yourself. I have taught you, time and time again, that it's not enough for you alone to find happiness. When you enter the path of the Middle Way and find happiness for yourself, know that this happiness is not given to you alone. You should share the happiness that you have found on the Middle Way with everyone around you. Your happiness must become the power to bring salvation to those around you.

My people, think of a canal when you ponder the concept of the Middle Way. If the canal only ran along the borders of the fields, then the water would not be able to reach all parts of the fields. Because the canal penetrates through the center of the fields, it can deliver much love to others. The canal always runs through the center, as if to cultivate the fields, and in turn, the fields flourish around it. Water is as blood to the fields, and canals are like veins that circulate the blood. The heart that pumps this blood through the veins is your loving heart. Do not forget this analogy.

My beloved disciples, I tell you that successful people are like canals running through fields. The canal runs straight across the fields, carrying and dispersing plenty of clean water. There is no virtue in the accumulation of water itself; neither goodness nor success is born from it. However, when you release that water into the canal and let it flow into a great many fields, it becomes virtuous; it becomes good; it becomes success. This is the path of a successful person.

Successful people are allowed to stay successful because they have given love to a great many people. If you yield a great harvest and keep it to yourself, others may envy or criticize you. But if you share the fruit, rice, and wheat that you have harvested, others will rejoice in the bounty of your great harvest. In sharing your success, your existence will become love itself; it will become goodness itself. This is the very essence of success. You are making a grave mistake if you seek to use the fruits of your success only for yourself. If you seek to serve a great many people with your fruition, your success will enrich the world and bring joy to the souls of many people.

Aspire to do the work of a canal. You must become a great pump that keeps pumping water into the canal when the fields are dry. The infinite water that wells up from the ground is equivalent to the light of Buddha. It is His compassion. You must learn how to receive His total love. When you wholeheartedly try to give love to others, to fill their hearts with love, you will find that the power, love, courage, and light of Buddha spring from within you, just as water gushes forth from underground. Believe that this will happen. This is what you must aspire to do. This is precisely what it means to live an ideal life.

THE PATH OF CULTIVATING YOURSELF

My people, listen well. You must also reserve a piece of that expansive land that spreads before you for the cultivation of yourself. Spare some time in your life to cultivate yourself. Set aside a certain amount of time each day, each month, and each year for your study. The time will not be futile, for you shall use it to build a canal that will become the groundwork to nurture many people.

What is the best way to cultivate yourself? It is to learn the everlasting Truths, which are the true knowledge that surpasses all other knowledge. Place the Truths at the center of your learning. Base your cultivation on the Truths. From the perspective of the Truths, restudy all the knowledge that you have learned and reexamine all the experiences that you have gained. Find experiences that shine like diamonds. Embellish yourself with fragments of the wisdom contained in your past studies. Fervently pursue and absorb whatever has the sense or aroma of the Truths.

To walk on the path to cultivation is to place the Truths at the center of your learning and surround them with the legacies of humankind, that is to say, the inventions, discoveries and innovations. People have made countless discoveries and generated innumerable innovations, ideas, and opinions over the course of history. You must sift all of them through the sieve of the Truths and nourish your soul with what remains in the sieve.

Cultivating yourself is like building a canal. A canal requires levees or dikes around it to carry water. At first glance, levees may seem to obstruct the flow of water. People may criticize you for building walls to control the flow of water. But think about it care-fully. What would happen if the canal did not run perfectly straight in the fields? What would happen if water simply gushed from the pump house directly into the fields? One part of the field would be drenched and flooded. Think about whether this would really help grow the seedlings. You know that it would not. Those tender seed-lings would drown in the pools of water and perhaps rot away.

This parable tells us that, in order to give love impartially to a great many, you need to build the groundwork of your life. You may have doubts as you build a flume. You may receive criticism during its construction. People may ridicule you as they watch you silently dig your canal, pour cement, and prepare to run water. Some will surely say, "You are a fool. Even if you build that canal, you won't get a single grain of rice or wheat from that land. You are wasting your time. You are only building that useless canal for your own satisfac-tion." However, you should silently continue your work. No matter what they say, you should never doubt your aspiration or forget your ideals. You will be able to achieve your grand plan someday.

Do not get caught up in what is immediately before you. Do not get trapped by the lure of immediate benefits. Your grand ideals should not shrink in the face of other people's criticism and back-biting. You need to keep building your canal straight and true. So long as your ultimate goal is to deliver Divine Love, you must never give up on building your canal. Once you have finished building your canal and it becomes useful, people will understand why you worked so hard on it. Until then, you may hear many critical words and questions about why you are building a canal. But you must remember that these are the words of people who do not compre-hend your ideals.

My beloved disciples, do you understand the lesson that I am trying to teach you through this analogy of the canal? Do you understand the true meaning of this parable? My eternal disciples, I am trying to teach you that you will have much to learn as you walk on the path to human perfection. You must cultivate yourself. You must walk the path of learning. Educating yourself is not easy, because it will require constant, untiring effort. As you accumulate knowledge, people may criticize you and tell you, "It's useless to study. Studying will do you no good." But the truth is that cultivating yourself opens a grand path that will provide you with sustenance for your soul. Walking on this path will help your soul grow. You are now building a canal that runs through an expansive plot of land. With this canal, you can water the arid lands and transform them into bountiful fields.

To be victorious in life and to guide many people, you must cultivate yourself; you must become cultured. This means gaining a great deal of knowledge and experience and then refining this knowledge and experience into something more precious. Learning random facts is not necessarily the same as becoming truly cultured. To become cultured, your knowledge needs to be accompanied by love. It is the catalyst of love that transforms knowledge into culture. What matters, therefore, is why you want to acquire knowledge. If your purpose for acquiring knowledge is to shine a spotlight on yourself and to show others how great you are, then your knowledge will never become culture. But if you seek knowledge out of a desire to benefit and nurture other people, then that knowledge will become a part of you. It will enrich your character and bring out your true potential. When you add the catalyst of love, you can turn your knowledge into wisdom; that is when you are truly walking on the path of learning.

By now, you see that walking on the path of the Middle Way may not be so easy. My beloved disciples, you must not lament the hardships you bear while walking on the path of improvement, the road of constant effort. Believe that this road is a golden road. Absorb spiritual nourishment and train your soul every day. Improving yourself to become a greater soul every day is the true purpose of your life. This is the true value of your life.

My people, from now on, make constant effort with untiring perseverance. Engrave your heart with the many lessons that you've learned, for this is how you will walk the path of diligence. I have taught Right Effort in my teaching of the Eightfold Path. Many people today may not understand what Right Effort truly means, but I say to you that the path of Right Effort will infinitely refine your character. It is an eternal path that leads to Buddha. You must never give up on walking this path. Even if you fall down, exhausted, you must never turn back. Even if you are unable to move forward any more, do not look back. Stay where you are, and take a short rest. Rest until your strength returns, and then resume your journey on the path of improvement. This is a great mission that has been entrusted onto you.

The Laws are powerless unless they are used to improve humankind. To make them truly empowering, those who learn them must muster courage, fill themselves with wisdom, and walk the path of improvement with hope. You must walk this path of improvement, for this path will take you to your ultimate goal of enlightenment.

II. Discarding the Poisons of the Mind

WHAT IS IGNORANCE?

Take a look around the world, and you'll see fools everywhere. Can you tell the difference between those who are ignorant and those who are not? You may try to distinguish between the two based on intelligence. But ignorance does not entirely depend on intellectual ability. It depends on a person's awareness of what his or her soul needs. Now take another look around you, this time paying attention to who lacks this sort of awareness. You will find that many people are indeed living the lives of fools, and you may even find that you yourself are one of them.

Living as a fool is like producing a poisonous toxin in your mind without even knowing what you are doing to yourself. You know that if you consume toxic food, your body will grow weak and eventually die. So why do you not realize that when you feed poison to your soul, you are killing it? Why do you not see what you are doing?

My people, listen carefully to my words. Without realizing it, each and every day, you are poisoning your soul. Each and every day, you are drinking arsenic. It may be just a small dose each day, but if you consume poison every day, it will accumulate inside you and will eventually kill your soul. What does it mean for your soul to die? It means that your soul will no longer possess the divine nature with which you were originally endowed. It means you will have resigned yourself to living in a way that contradicts the very purpose for which you were created.

KNOW YOUR TRUE SELF

One kind of foolishness is to not know oneself. Fools of this type are proud of themselves when they do not even know their true self. You may read tens of thousands of books and travel the entire world, but to be truly wise, you must understand your true nature. You may accumulate great knowledge, memorize much information, and visit many countries, but none of these will make you wise: to be truly wise, you must understand your own mind. Those who know and control their mind and awaken to their true self will become wise even if they lack worldly knowledge or experience.

My people, do not put the cart before the horse. You must begin your work by governing yourself. No matter how much money and time you spend and no matter how much help you receive from others, you will never be wise until you know and control yourself. You must know yourself well. Knowing yourself means knowing that you are a child of Buddha. The truly wise do not seek respect from others, for they realize that their bodies and souls have come from Him.

I say this again. You must know yourself well. Make this your first goal. To be truly wise, you must know yourself before you try to know the world and other people. No matter how much knowledge you accumulate, if you are not aware of your true nature, you will remain ignorant.

THE MIND OF OFFERING: AN ANTIDOTE TO GREED

My beloved disciples, I want to teach you about the poisons of the mind. You must begin by abandoning your greed. Do you know what a greedy mind is? It is a mind that constantly seeks to take. It is a mind that always desires more and more. A greedy mind might desire status, promotion, or fame. When you continuously covet, like a starving ghost that never gets full no matter how much it eats, your soul falls into an unfathomable depth of stagnation.

My people, you must deeply reflect on your mind. If you find a strong sense of greed there, you should know that you are a fool. Stop clinging to social status, career advancement, fame, and pride. It is a greedy mind that gives rise to the desire to be thought highly of, to be respected, to be admired, to become famous, and to exercise your authority over others. My people, if your mind is poisoned with greed, immediately take hold of the greed and discard it from your mind. You must not allow it to enter your mind again. Shut the door of your mind and never again grant it access to your heart.

Do you understand why greed is a poison for your mind? Do you know why it is evil? Greed is poisonous because it disrupts your gentleness. To be gentle is a noble thing. A gentle facial expression, kind words, and a soft attitude are all precious, for it is in this gentleness that you will find Buddha.

My people, the enlightened ones are always serene. The enlightened ones walk meekly, with a smile. The enlightened ones do not swagger. The enlightened ones are not arrogant. The enlightened ones do not show off, judge others, or try to harm others. The enlightened ones are gentle, polite, poised, and graceful.

My beloved disciples, you must know that it is not easy for souls to be granted life and to be born into this world. You were given a rare chance to be born in this era and encounter the teachings of Buddha. You have been given a precious opportunity to live in the same age as Buddha, at a time when a living Buddha expounds his teachings. When you realize how few souls have had the chance to be born in this era, your mission in life will become clear: you were born to give to others.

"To give" is a modern term that expresses the mind of offering. A mind of offering is a mind that cares for others. It is a mind that wishes good things for others. It is a mind that serves others. If you do not have a mind of offering, then the teachings of Buddha will be meaningless. The teachings of Buddha are meant to help you serve others, give to others, and love others.

BE KIND, NOT SELFISH

Another kind of foolishness is to lack kindness in one's heart. Some people do not realize how important it is to be kind. Those who lack kindness in their hearts think nothing of shoving people aside, asserting superiority, and demanding obedience. These people are not aware of the tremendous life mistakes they are making. To be kind is to help others feel happy to be alive. Having kindness in your heart is the greatest proof that you are a child of Buddha.

True kindness leads to true sorrow. Many of your fellow human beings are experiencing great pain and suffering. Bound by their physical limitations, faced with many impediments to enlightenment, with few chances to attain spiritual awakening, they live lives of suffering. Animals and plants are suffering as well. When you see all the pain and suffering that fills this world, when you see the thorns that pierce people, it's only natural to want to remove the pain. To feel the pain and sadness of others and shed tears for them is to have great compassion, or as I sometime say, great sorrow. These are the tears of Buddha's mercy.

My people, when you no longer feel sad for others, you become self-centered. You begin to think only about yourself and your own happiness; you focus on your own sorrow. But thinking about your own sorrow will not help you improve the world. To create a better world, you must remove the thorns and poisonous stings from the hearts of others. This is the mindset you should have. So remember to keep looking at the world around you. Look at the people, animals, and plants. Feel their sadness. Their sadness will tell you what this moment requires of you.

Those who think only of their own happiness and their own protection put forth untiring effort to benefit themselves, but the direction of their efforts is the opposite of the will of Buddha. They do not understand that by seeking only to benefit themselves, they are actually harming themselves. They do not understand that they were not born to be selfish. Neither were you born to devote your life solely to yourself. You have been blessed with unparalleled compassion to have been born into this world today. Be grateful for this precious opportunity, and devote your life to quenching the thirsty hearts of many people. Do not think too much about yourself. Do not think only of your own happiness.

Long ago, I taught you that your efforts to benefit yourself must not bring harm to others. You should never wish to hurt or harm others. Your efforts to benefit yourself must always benefit others as well. When you take good control of yourself, govern your mind, and polish your soul, you will enter a wonderful world. Your efforts to refine yourself should help others improve themselves and help make this world that Buddha has created a more wonderful place. Do not misinterpret the meaning of benefiting yourself.

BEAUTIFY YOUR MIND BEFORE BEAUTIFYING YOUR BODY

Do not be overly concerned about your physical appearance. Do not trouble yourself with whether you are too tall or short, too fat or thin, attractive or unattractive. Do not become obsessed by your outward appearance to the point that you find yourself talking about it every day. Only the ignorant fret about these issues. The body is nothing but a vehicle for your soul. It is enough that your body fulfills its purpose as a vehicle for your soul training in this lifetime. Do not desire any more than that. Do not be distressed by your physical body or worry about your appearance. Instead, think about your mind. What's on your mind? If your mind is filled with wrong thoughts, that should concern you more than your physical appearance. Consider whether your mind is beautiful or not. Worry about whether your heart is pure and beautiful.

Your heart will manifest itself in your physical appearance. If your mind is beautiful, that beauty will be reflected in your eyes. If your mind is impure, your eyes will be cloudy, gleam with a vicious light, or give off malevolent vibrations. The nose of an arrogant person will indeed seem stuck up and pointy. The mouth of a person whose mind is evil will appear crooked. The lips of those who always make sarcastic remarks and criticize others will appear pursed and bent. A disturbed mind will appear in one's demeanor—those who constantly blame and torment others will carry themselves in a way that corresponds with those traits.

Those with a peaceful mind will make you forget the time you are living in. They will make you forget where you are. They will make you feel so quiet that you'll feel as though you are alone together even when you are surrounded by a crowd of people. This is because their minds are always gentle and serene. People with a meek and calm mind never cause discomfort to those around them.

My people, before you tone your body, attune your mind. Before beautifying your body, beautify your mind. Be gentle every day. Do not get angry. Do not speak ill of others. Do not grumble. Engrave these words into your mind.

RESPOND TO ANGER WITH GENTLENESS

Anger is another poison of the mind. You must not become angry. No matter what kind of humiliation you face, you must never become angry. This teaching is vital, especially for spiritual seekers. During the course of your spiritual discipline, you may be criticized, and you may be insulted. But as disciples of Buddha, you must endure these humiliations. You must not repay anger with anger. You must respond with gentle words. You must answer harsh criticisms with silence. Remember to smile. Remember to practice endurance and patience. Remember to persevere, for this discipline will make you virtuous. To acquire virtue, you will need endurance. To be virtuous, you will need to respond to anger with gentleness, not with more anger. You must never, ever give in to anger.

BE LOVING AND RESPECTFUL, NOT ENVIOUS

Envy is the most dangerous poison for those on the path to enlightenment. Once the poison of envy enters you, it instantly nullifies everything you've acquired through your decades of spiritual discipline. All the virtue that you have accumulated vanishes instantaneously.

Do not be envious or jealous of others. You must be very careful about this, for it is another essential teaching for spiritual seekers. As you practice your discipline, you may hear good things about others; you may hear that someone else has reached a higher state of mind. This may momentarily evoke jealousy in you, but you must not give in to your jealous feelings. Harboring feelings of envy and jealousy is a foolish way to live. Do not live this way.

Envy is evil because it does not make anyone happy. It brings unhappiness to both the envious person and the person who is envied. Envy disrupts the harmony and peace of the mind. Now that you understand that envy is evil, you must never be envious.

If you meet people of high caliber, love them, respect them, and honor them. You can become like them only by honoring those who are greater than you. Honoring people of high caliber is your first step on the path of progress. Love and revere these people. Love those who have talent, experience, and wisdom. This is essential.

DO NOT COMPLAIN; WORK DILIGENTLY AND SILENTLY

I have taught you that you must not get angry and that you must not become envious. The next poison that you must rid yourself of is the habit of complaining. People complain when they cannot satisfy their own desires. Complaints escalate to criticism and discontent; they then spread and permeate the minds of everyone around you. Avoiding a mindset of complaint is one of the important virtues for spiritual seekers to practice.

Complaint is poisonous. Like littered garbage, complaints harm and pollute those around you. Those who complain are creating a garbage dump all around them, surrounding themselves and others with mountains of trash. If you complain, who will clean up after you? Who will take out the trash that you are littering around you? You must clean up the mess you have made. Those who complain must dispose of their trash themselves. Otherwise, they have no choice but to live out their lives amid their mountain of trash. This is the most terrifying thing about complaint.

Do you know why you complain? Complaints are triggered by a lack of ability or a lack of self-confidence. When you feel a need to complain, you must encourage yourself. You must cheer yourself up. Tell yourself that you are a far greater person than that. Tell yourself that you were created by Divine Light. Divine Life resides within you. Encourage yourself to shine with a greater and brighter light. Your urge to complain will leave you.

You may also complain when you feel fatigued. This is a normal human tendency. But if you find yourself wanting to complain when you feel tired, you should instead remain silent. When you feel the need to complain, silence yourself and take a deep breath. Then strive to detach yourself from that thought as quickly as you can.

Some people complain because they cannot accomplish what they desire. Some of you may hold grudges because there are things that you know you cannot obtain, no matter how hard you work for them. But what good comes from complaining about it? Do you think complaining will help you progress toward your desires? Complaining is like trying desperately to paddle your boat into safe harbor, but your paddling creates waves of water that bounces off the shores and push you back farther away to sea. Complaining about your inability to accomplish something only pushes you farther away from your goal.

Instead of complaining, quietly store up power within you. Look toward the future and keep working diligently and silently. No one has ever succeeded without effort. You will not develop spiritually by experiencing easy success. Easy success is like a castle in the air: it will crumble in the end.

My people, do not spare pains. You cannot accomplish anything without diligent effort. You cannot achieve success without perseverance. If you've become successful without working for it, you should be ashamed of that success. You should be ashamed of that honor. You should be ashamed of that fame. It is the process of working hard, not the results of your hard work, that is your golden glory.

I have taught you that foolish people are those who get angry, envy others, and complain; this holds true in all ages. Look deep within yourself, and constantly examine whether you have anger, envy, or complaint in your mind. As long as you have any of these poisons in your mind, you are still ignorant. Cease to be foolish. Become wise, for this is the path to enlightenment.

DO NOT MISLEAD OTHERS; CULTIVATE HUMILITY

My people, I will tell you about another kind of fool. Fools of this kind find joy in drawing attention to themselves and causing panic and confusion. This kind of fool plants poison in the minds of others, makes them worry, lures them into the chasm of temptation, fabricates lies, spreads rumors, and deludes those who are working diligently on the path to enlightenment. From time to time, this type of fool appears among those who study my teachings. These people try to bring others down with them because they are frustrated with their slow progress toward enlightenment or because they haven't been given an important position in their order. They try to distract those who have dedicated themselves to spiritual discipline and tempt them to join the ranks of complainers and grumblers.

My people, you must know that this mindset and these thoughts and actions are in tune with the minds of those in Hell. The numerous lost souls living in Hell do not try to save themselves. Instead, they try to increase the number of fellow culprits. They try to assuage their own suffering by causing others to suffer, by trying to delude others as they have been deluded, or by dragging others into the pitfalls of desire. If they continue to act this way, they will never experience peace of mind. You must never become like them. Do not use others to lessen your own suffering. Do not lure others to your side. Do not complain or grumble to others. Your suffering is for you and you alone. You must confront your sufferings yourself. You must work out your problems within yourself. Never try to justify or rationalize your mistaken thoughts and actions by forming a faction with others.

I say to you that the most foolish people on Earth are the ones who seek to mislead those who have devoted themselves to the path to enlightenment. Thinking that they are correct and wise, and not recognizing that they are actually fools, these people distort and bend the teachings of Buddha based on their limited knowledge. They try to explain their insidious ideas in a way that serves themselves. This behavior paves the way to Hell. The wise understand how great a sin it is to think in this way. Those of you who follow and learn the Laws of the Truths must never bend or distort the teachings, spread incorrect teachings, or tempt others to follow you in an attempt to justify your wrong thoughts and actions. You, my wise people, must know that there is greed lurking at the bottom of this kind of think-ing: those who think in this way covet the authority and veneration of those who correctly preach the Laws.

My people, each and every person has his or her capacity. You must reach a certain level to become a true teacher. Those who, in the eternal process of reincarnation, have continuously refined their souls and achieved great feats shall walk ahead of others and lead those who follow. But those who are mentally or spiritually underde-veloped or simply still have a lot to learn must follow the guidance of a teacher. No matter what age you are born into, people are always at different stages of spiritual progress. To learn well, you must know your place. To gain greater knowledge, you must humble yourself. To attain greater enlightenment, you must control yourself well.

DO NOT FEAR LONELINESS; EMBRACE THE TIME OF SOLITUDE

My beloved disciples, as you walk on this path to enlightenment, you need to keep a strong mind. Prepare yourself to endure this long journey alone. Be prepared for loneliness. Develop your ability to bear this hardship, for this ability is the key to victory in life. You must endure loneliness before you can achieve true success, for true success requires a time of solitude. A time of gaiety may come later, but loneliness; always precedes success. How you live through these times of solitude determines your success.

Sometimes the time of solitude lasts only a short time, but some-times it lasts a very long time. It may last ten or twenty years. But you must not fear loneliness; do not forget that in times of solitude, Buddha is always beside you. When you are sitting alone, do not forget that the Supreme Being is sitting right next to you. You are not alone. The time of solitude does not visit you just for the sake of loneliness; it visits you to train your soul. In times of loneliness you will find a great chance to develop your soul. Your soul is about to shed light. Light is about to shine from the depths of your soul.

Young ones, do not fear loneliness, for enduring a time of solitude challenges you to become a person of authenticity. Young ones, seek not only gaiety. Seek not only a life of joviality. Do not only desire the attention and praise of others. Find something that will keep improving you for all eternity. Grasp something that will nurture you eternally. The moment you take hold of it, you will undergo a great transformation. You will not be able to remain the same. You will see a complete 180-degree change. You will encounter divine time, divine moment, and divine being. You become truly valiant only when you overcome loneliness.

DO NOT BE IMPATIENT; WALK YOUR PATH QUIETLY

I have always taught you to rid yourself of attachments. The biggest attachment that will prevent you from achieving success is your attachment to time. Your attachment to time is called *impatience*. You constantly suffer from this attachment. You are constantly trapped by the delusions of this attachment. You are constantly made a prisoner of it. Have you ever thought about the nature of impatience? You become impatient when you desire to see results quickly. Impatience is a desire to obtain results and reach a goal without making sufficient effort.

My people, impatience is an enemy of life. Those who walk quietly shall travel far. Those who travel silently shall go a great distance. But those who sound their bells and pound their drums shall not progress very far on their journey, for masses of people will be drawn to the festive sounds and will wish to speak with the traveler. As the traveler engages in conversation, he will soon forget the original purpose of his journey. Thus, my people, if you wish to move quickly on your journey, you must go quietly. If your destination lies far ahead, you must go swiftly, silently, and in a state of deep reflection. Do not be hasty. Do not rush.

My people, remember these words deep in your hearts. In life, if you ever find your mind wavering, ask yourself if it is your impatience that is causing your troubles, worries, and uncertainty. In these moments, take a deep breath and ask yourself why you are feeling impatient. Why are you in such a hurry? Why are you rushing? As you ponder these questions, you will realize that your impatience lacks a solid foundation; there is no real reason for you to be troubled at all. There is usually no real reason to move hastily. In most cases, a feeling of haste is caused by the shadows of fear. As you move forward on your journey, you develop a vague anxiety that something terrible is going to happen to you in the future. The source of haste is the fear that something harmful will stand in your way.

My people, ponder deeply your mission in life, the purpose of your life. Then you will realize that you were not born on Earth to live your life as quickly as possible. If you sprint right through life, you will never be able to savor it. It is not truly important to reach the highest peaks of worldly success. Do not fear that your life is uneventful. Do not fear that your life is ordinary. Do not be swayed by temporary trends. Do not give in to the commonly accepted ideas of this world. Do not let the opinions of others agitate you.

Those who follow the path should do so silently. Those who pursue the path should go quietly. Do not let others hear the sound of your footsteps. You do not need to tell others that you are leaving for a long journey. No, you must not let others know, because if you do, some may try to stop you, not out of malice, but out of good will. One after another, they will advise you not to go because of the dangers the journey may involve. You must not get distracted, even by those who claim to love you dearly.

III. *Success on the Path to Enlightenment*

As you walk the path to enlightenment, you are probably finding yourself powerfully drawn to success. You are probably longing for success every day. But you are probably also thinking about what success is. The true definition of success may be very different from what you envision. Success may be much closer to you than you would ever have imagined. There is no fixed definition of success, but I will tell you the conditions that you must keep in mind as you work toward true success.

SUCCESS REQUIRES A PEACEFUL MIND

It is not true success if it disturbs your mind. Thus, the first condition of success is that your mind must always remain peaceful. Your mind must always be calm and poised. Your mind must always be serene and free of attachments. If your success makes you increasingly attached to worldly desires, then that success is not genuine. True success makes your mind more peaceful and serene. It brings richness to your mind and leads you to think and care about many people. Only if you feel this serenity, richness, and compassion is your success true success.

SUCCESS DOES NOT INCUR JEALOUSY

It is not true success if, in the process of attaining success, you create conflict and struggle or incur resentment and jealousy. Therefore, the second condition of success is not to incur jealousy. There has not been a single person who has achieved true success while incurring other people's jealousy. Some people who appear to have found success will eventually sink into the chasm of ruin because they have invited others' jealousy along the way. If you have evoked envy, it means that you have gained your success by pushing others aside. It means that you have attained your success by standing on the shoulders of others. It means that you have achieved your success by making other people carry your heaviest burdens.

If the purpose of your success is to help lift others' burdens, add comfort to their lives, and bring them happiness, then your success will never incur jealousy or resentment. But if even one person envies your success, then you must know that you are lacking virtue, that you are not yet a virtuous person. What does it mean to be lacking in virtue? It means that your success has caused others to think either that they have suffered a loss or that your success is undeserved. They do not approve of your success. This is not the sort of success you should pursue.

True success is naturally supported and upheld by everyone around you. True success isn't something that you can achieve by pursuing your own individual ambition; rather, it is something that emerges naturally from practicing virtue and following your spiritual path with dedication. True success makes everyone around you thankful. Know that true success brings widespread gratitude.

SUCCESS CARRIES THE FRAGRANCE OF ENLIGHTENMENT

I now share with you the third condition of success. In addition to maintaining a peace of mind and an attitude that does not arouse jealousy in others, you need to increase the radiance of your soul as you succeed. Do you understand what I mean by this? It means that you must carry a fragrance of enlightenment. You must give off an aroma of enlightenment.

But you cannot gain the fragrance of enlightenment simply by wanting it. You can never possess it by trying to seize it. You can obtain it when you don't seek it; you can gain it without desiring it. It is like a butterfly: when you chase it around with your net, it escapes and flies higher, but when you stand still and quietly wait, it floats down and lands on your shoulder. In the same way, enlightenment comes naturally, contrary to your will. Its mellow fragrance enriches your mind and the minds of all those around you.

Enlightenment does not exist in a world beyond your ordinary life; nor does it exist outside of your usual experiences. Rather, you can find hints of enlightenment within your ordinary, everyday life. This is where the path to enlightenment begins. And the enlightenment that you find in your ordinary life consists of small discoveries that you make in each ordinary day.

What does it mean to make small discoveries in your life? You make these discoveries when, in the course of leading your life, you remember the music that filled your heart when you were in Heaven. You must recall the melody that you enjoyed in the other world. What is the music of Heaven? It is your affection for others, feeling happy for other people's happiness, and the contentment that arises when you discard your strong desires. It is also a mind that seeks harmony, cooperation, and nurture of one another. It is a selfless mind that pursues more than your own happiness and your own selfish desires. It is a pure mind filled with feelings that are infinitely transparent, kind, and warm.

This is the world of Heaven. Remember the world of Heaven every day, as you live your life in this world. Picture your life in Heaven in your mind every day. Live every day with an image of this peaceful world in your mind all the time. This will enable you to control your mind; your mind will no longer be your enemy, but will be your ally that will heed your every command and serve as a very important force.

SUCCESS IS THE FRUIT OF PATIENCE AND PERSEVERANCE

I have told you how to attain this third condition of success, the fragrance of enlightenment, in the course of ordinary life. It is life's ordinariness that makes patience so important. Patience may not play a large role in the extraordinary days of an extraordinary life, but it takes great patience to continue living each and every ordinary day. Living an ordinary life requires extraordinary patience. It is a very trying and difficult task to live an ordinary life while recalling your memories of Heaven and trying to turn them into reality, but persevering in these efforts will lead you to progress eternally.

It is nearly impossible to attain enlightenment in an instant. It is difficult to make great spiritual progress all at once. The key to opening a bright future is to take one step forward every day, day after day. Even if you cannot read an entire book, even if you can only read a single line in a day, you will move forward if you continue your efforts every day.

You need perseverance to attain success. The success you achieve based on perseverance will not incur jealousy, for people will respect all the effort you have put into accomplishing it. Success achieved through continual effort always shines with virtue. Virtue is an antidote that can completely erase jealousy and envy from the minds of others. To be truly successful, you must acquire virtue through perseverance; your efforts will surely be rewarded. You will receive even more than you expected, and others will also receive the blessings of your virtue.

AUTHOR'S THOUGHTS

THE FOUNDATIONS OF SHAKYAMUNI BUDDHA'S TEACHINGS

Considering that Shakyamuni Buddha lived about 2,500 years ago, it is truly incredible that he expounded such a refined and lofty philosophy that is still taught today. One of Shakyamuni Buddha's fundamental teachings is that as we live in this material world, each of us must find our true self, the spiritual self that resides in the other world. He taught that the objective of meditation is to remember what it was like in the world of Heaven. He also taught that we should ponder how to think and act so we can live a better life—one that accords with the Truths. These were the foundations of what Shakyamuni preached for forty-five years. So rich and diverse were Shakyamuni's teachings that it is said that he offered eighty-four thousand different teachings. However, the main pillars of Shakyamuni's teachings can be summarized under the following five pillars.

THE FIRST PILLAR: THE RELATIONSHIP BETWEEN THIS WORLD AND THE OTHER WORLD

The first pillar is the relationship between the spirit world and the physical world that we live in. Shakyamuni taught that human beings have eternal life and reside in the spirit world before birth and after death. The three-dimensional world is simply a reflection of the spirit world, which was created by the will of the Primordial Buddha (Primordial God). So the material world we live in is like a shadow of the spirit world. The majority of people are under the illusion that this world of shadow, this temporary abode, is the only world that exists, so they cling to it desperately, bringing much misery upon themselves as a result. We can free ourselves from this anguish by remembering the other world where we all originated. This way, we are able to cast off our attachments to our material selves and find our true selves. This is how we can cast aside the sufferings of birth, aging, and illness. All that will remain before us is a world of joy as we become dazzling manifestations of light. This is the first pillar of Shakyamuni's teachings; we can think of this pillar as his theory of space.

THE SECOND PILLAR: THE LAW OF CAUSE AND EFFECT

The second pillar of Shakyamuni's teachings is his theory of time. The key to this pillar is his concept of temporal causation: the law of cause and effect that is at work both in this world and the other world. Shakyamuni taught that there is a cause for every effect and that if you want to change the effect, you need to change the cause. The relationship between cause and effect ties events together, connects people, and gives birth to everything in the universe. Human beings are subject to the law of reincarnation in the eternal flow of time, and this cycle of birth is also governed by the law of cause and effect.

The tendencies of your soul and the environment you were born into were determined by your thoughts and actions in a previous life. In the same way, the world you will return to and the kind of life you will lead in the next life depends on your life in the present life. To put it another way, you are assured of a glorious next life if you live a virtuous life this time. If you want to break out of the vicious circle of fate that seems to assail you, you have no choice but to make diligent efforts to rebuild your present life. This is what emancipation really means. Enlightenment is about discovering our true self, the self that is adamantine and unshakable to the vagaries of fate. Moreover, if we achieve the state of *tathagata* through enlightenment, we can free ourselves from the shackles of reincarnation ruled by the law of causality. At that point, we become able to voluntarily be born into this world. This is the second pillar of Shakyamuni's philosophy.

THE THIRD PILLAR: THE EIGHTFOLD PATH

The third pillar of Shakyamuni's teachings is the Eightfold Path, which is a path to human perfection that measures our spiritual development. As soon as human beings are born into this world, we forget everything about the other world. Because most of our accumulated knowledge remains hidden in our subconscious, we have to depend on our limited surface consciousness as we go through our lives in this world. We have a lot of information stored in our deeper consciousness, which exists in the other world, but the only way we can sense this information is by paying attention to the inspirations we receive and the patterns of thought and action that represent the tendencies of our souls.

Worldly desires that spring from materialistic values separate our surface consciousness from our subconscious. Worldly desires are negative mental functions, formed since birth by distorted environments, education, thoughts, beliefs, habits, and actions. We have to discard our worldly desires to find our true selves and to regain 100 percent of our latent capabilities. To do this, we need to look back on our lives, up to the present day, find the causes of the disharmony in our minds, and repent our misdeeds one by one. The criteria we should use for this introspection are laid down in the Eightfold Path, which consists of Right View, Right Thought, Right Speech, Right Action, Right Livelihood, Right Effort, Right Mindfulness, and Right Concentration.

First, ask yourself whether you have viewed the events you have experienced and the people you've met from the right perspective, that is, one based on faith. (Right View)

Second, ask if you have held right thoughts. See whether your thoughts have been pure and clear or unruly, disarrayed, and impure. Would you feel ashamed if your thoughts were visible to other people, as if they were put in a transparent box? (Right Thought)

Third, ask yourself if you've spoken rightly. Most of our suffering is caused by careless remarks and the negative words of others or ourselves. Check whether you have spoken the right words. (Right Speech)

Fourth, have you acted right and devoted yourself to your work? Your occupation is your mission, given by Buddha, and a service of gratitude. Are you really fulfilling your calling? (Right Action)

Fifth, have you lived right? Do you consider your life in this world a time of spiritual training? Do you live each day fully, as if it were your last? Have you lived in harmony, drawing on the Truths as food for your soul? (Right Livelihood)

Sixth, have you made right efforts? Have you walked on the right path as a child of Buddha? Have you studied the Truths and striven to improve yourself? (Right Effort)

Seventh, have you been able to make an appropriate plan for your life? Do you pray rightly to Buddha? Do you always strive to achieve self-realizations that would not make you feel ashamed even if you were to present them directly to Buddha? (Right Mindfulness)

Finally, have you taken the time for right meditation? The true goal of meditation is not to empty your mind, but to receive from Heaven the light of Buddha and the guidance of your guardian and guiding spirits. This is an indispensable form of study for all seekers of the Truth. (Right Concentration)

The Eightfold Path is the third pillar of Shakyamuni's teachings. He taught his followers to reflect on their past based on the Eightfold Path so that they could build a bright future.

THE FOURTH PILLAR: THE SIX PARAMITAS

The fourth pillar of Shakyamuni's teachings is his philosophy of the Six Paramitas, or six perfections.* The Six Paramitas are teachings that develop the self while improving our relationships with others. Shakyamuni taught that we can attain enlightenment by achieving these six perfections. Shakyamuni's teachings of the Six Paramitas are as follows:

1. Dana Paramita

This is the perfection of offering, which is a manifestation of mercy. It refers to a mindset of wishing to save others through both material and spiritual charity. This idea corresponds to the Christian teaching of love.

2. Sila Paramita

This is the perfection of observing the five precepts: Do not kill, do not steal, do not commit adultery, do not speak falsely, and do not drink to the extent that it ruins your life.

3. Ksanti Paramita

This is the perfection of perseverance. To qualify as a seeker of the Truths, you cannot react to other people's wrath or be angered by their unreasonable words and actions. Even if you have a good rea-

---

* The Sanskrit word "parami" means inherent wisdom, while "ta" refers to the way this wisdom overflows.

son to be upset, taking in their poison attunes you to the vibrations of Hell. But if you remain calm and let anger pass, then slander, jealousy, and anger will simply bounce off you and return to the person who harbored them and sent them your way. This is the law of action and reaction.

4. Virya Paramita
This is the perfection of effort. To understand and acquire the Truths, seekers must work diligently every day.

5. Dhyana Paramita
This is the perfection of meditation, which aims to commune with the spirits in the other world.

6. Prajna Paramita
This is the perfection of wisdom, which lies at the very heart of Shakyamuni's teachings. In the spirit world, Shakyamuni's soul casts the golden light of wisdom. He is the Great Guiding Spirit of Light whose mission is to intellectually explain the entire structure and system of the Laws. He holds the key to the reservoir of wisdom in the spirit world.

The teachings of the Six Paramitas are similar to the Eightfold Path, and they overlap in some ways. Some people believe that the Eightfold Path is a teaching of Theravada Buddhism while the Six Paramitas are mainly taught in Mahayana Buddhism. But the two teachings simply correspond to different levels of enlightenment. While the Eightfold Path was a training method for *arhats*, that is, those at the threshold of becoming bodhisattvas, the Six Paramitas are practices that help bodhisattvas become *tathagatas*. You cannot become a bodhisattva without understanding the concept of charity or giving love to others, and you cannot become a *tathagata* without having awakened to wisdom. Both love and wisdom are necessary to become a *tathagata*.

THE FIFTH PILLAR: THE CONCEPT OF EMPTINESS

The fifth pillar of Shakyamuni's teachings is the idea of emptiness or void (*shunyata in* Sanskrit), which has been a topic of discussion for more than two thousand years. What is the meaning of the famous Buddhist expression "Matter is void—void is matter"? To understand this, you need to understand that Divine Light brings about creation and destruction through the processes of condensation and diffusion.

All material objects in this world are made of condensed particles of Divine Light that take certain shapes according to the will or intention of their spiritual energy. Material objects in this world are made up of particles, which are formed by molecules, which are created by atoms, which appear when photons are gathered for a particular purpose. Since the photons are concentrated energy created by Divine Will, if His will were to disappear, these photons would cease to exist. This means that everything—including all existence in the third dimension, the fourth dimension, and the higher dimensions—ceases to exist the moment He stops willing us into existence. This is the true meaning of his teaching, "Matter is void—void is matter." This is the true meaning of Shakyamuni Buddha's concept of emptiness.

SHAKYAMUNI BUDDHA INTEGRATED DIVERSE VALUES

Shakyamuni Buddha would never have been fully satisfied to occupy himself only with practical affairs. But by examining the path he took as a spiritual leader, we can clearly see that he was gifted with exceptional practical intelligence. He formed a *sangha*—a self-governing community of monks and nuns. In much the same way that governments pass legislation, Shakyamuni established precepts to maintain order among his followers. He created a quasi-judicial system that functioned as the sangha's internal court or council and established precepts to guide this system. He built temples in different areas to act as bases of various activities, and he also saw to their management. He received offerings from kings, and recruited powerful followers from among the laity. These historical facts demonstrate just how gifted Shakyamuni was for managing practical affairs. He was certainly too gifted to live out his days in Shakya, one small country out of the sixteen countries that made up the India of that time. This gifted man founded Buddhism, a religion that is still practiced to this day.

Shakyamuni embodied and integrated two extreme characteristics: he was very strict but also very tolerant. He was very rational and logical but also had a sentimental side; he was very sensitive to the feelings of others, and his value for compassion reflects this sensitivity. Furthermore, he had a highly intelligent, practical mind, but also developed deep mystical insights.

Shakyamuni certainly was a philosopher, and his teachings are difficult to fully understand. He delved into the truths of the spirit world much more deeply than any other philosopher, and he taught the true meanings of happiness and unhappiness from a spiritual perspective.

Like its founder, Buddhism is a fusion of rationality and mysticism, and its modern-day revival must incorporate both of these orientations. True Buddhism must seek to build a world where people with genuine faith can open a path to the future by working diligently and recognizing the mysteries of the great universe, the world created by the Primordial Buddha (Primordial God). Buddhism must teach that building such a world will give rise to the ideal society.

CHAPTER 3

MOSES

Righteousness Must Prevail

THE LIFE OF MOSES

MOSES'S CHILDHOOD

Long ago, when God decided to begin creating a kingdom of God on Earth, He dispatched Moses, a great leader from the ninth dimension of Heaven, to Egypt. When Moses descended to Earth, he was born to Hebrew slaves. Soon after birth, however, he was set adrift in a reed basket on the Nile River. Fortunately, the pharaoh's daughter found him and took him back to the palace, where she raised him and provided him with an education in academics and military arts. Moses suffered from deep heartache when, at the age of eighteen, he discovered the truth about his birth parents. He could not stand the thought that if fortune had not been on his side, he would have been one of the vast number of suffering slaves who were working on the construction of the city of Ramses, which was being built to commemorate Ramses II (1292–1225 BCE). For many years, Moses devoted himself to his studies while patiently waiting for the day that he would be able to free his people.

When Moses was twenty-seven, he had an unforgettable experience. He was out in the fields herding sheep when he suddenly saw a pillar of flame in the distance. As he walked toward it, he heard a voice say: "I am that I am.* I existed before all else."

And he also heard a voice say:

---

* As I once explained, during a lecture in Hawaii, it was El Cantare who told Moses, "I am that I am."

I am the God of Abraham, the God of Isaac, the God of Jacob-Israel. I am the Lord of all the armies; I am Yahweh. Save my people in Egypt. Listen to the sorrows of my people. Moses, free my people, deliver them out of Egypt, and take them to the land flowing with milk and honey. Lead them to Canaan and build the nation of Israel. For this end have I selected you.

THE EXODUS

When Moses was thirty-five, seventeen years after he learned of his birth parents, an opportunity to lead his people out of Egypt arrived. The exodus was a kind of coup d'etat against the pharaoh Merneptah (1225–1215 BCE). Moses's rebel army grew in force as increasing numbers of slaves were freed. Eventually, the number of able-bodied men in Moses's army swelled to six hundred thousand people, but Moses did not want to fight the pharaoh. His only purpose was to guide the Hebrew people out of Egypt to found their own kingdom. Therefore, to avoid causing riots, Moses gathered his people and began the exodus from Egypt.

Guided by the voice of Yahweh, who is also sometimes called Jehovah, Moses led two million men, women, and children out of Egypt. However, just as they reached the Red Sea, the pharaoh's armies came after them in hot pursuit. So Moses built an altar by the sea and prayed to Yahweh: "O my Lord, I have led the Hebrew nation out of Egypt as you commanded, but our way forward is blocked by the sea, and the king's army is at our heels. We have nowhere to turn, and I do not have ships to carry our people. If I fight the pharaoh's army, many of our people will be killed or wounded. Please, O Lord of armies, save us from our enemies."

Yahweh answered, "Moses, why are you afraid? There is nothing in this world that I do not control. The wind, the trees, the mountains, the rivers, and the sky are all at my command. Where is this sea that you fear? For the sake of my people, I will sunder it apart." As the story goes, no sooner had Yahweh spoken than an unbelievable phenomenon took place before the eyes of Moses and the Hebrews: two kilometers of sea split apart, leaving a path twenty meters wide across the sea floor. The waters reared to a height of fifteen meters on either side and then fell back as if an invisible wall was holding the two sides apart. Here and there along the newly formed path, red and blue fish of various sizes flopped around helplessly on the sea floor. "Hurry!" cried Moses, and the Hebrew people hurried forward. As soon as they reached the other side, the sea walls came crashing down. Part of Pharaoh's army ran back to shore; the rest drowned.

Later, on top of Mt. Sinai, Yahweh appeared before Moses and revealed to him the Ten Commandments:

1. *You shall have no other gods before me.*
2. *You shall not make any graven images.*
3. *You shall not take the name of the Lord your God in vain.*
4. *You shall remember the Sabbath day and keep it holy.*
5. *You shall honor your father and mother.*
6. *You shall not kill.*
7. *You shall not commit adultery.*
8. *You shall not steal.*
9. *You shall not bear false witness against your neighbor.*
10. *You shall not covet your neighbor's house.*

The first four commandments are religious, the fifth is moral, and the sixth through the tenth are ethical and legal precepts. The Ten Commandments have had a tremendous influence all over the world. Monotheism began with the emergence of the Ten Commandments and it is because of the Ten Commandments that so many people believe in a unique, personal God who provides divine laws to create social order.

The god that the Israelites called Yahweh was actually Enlil, a spirit from Heaven. It was the ethnic god Enlil who commanded Moses to build the nation of Israel. But it was Elohim (also known as El), a god who had been worshiped throughout the Middle East since ancient times, who said to Moses, "I am that I am." This was the beginning of the confusion between Enlil and El, the Supreme Being that we now know as El Cantare. This confusion between different gods was the cause of Israel's history of isolation, fierce wars, and three thousand years of persecution. It is unfortunate that Moses's inability to differentiate between the Supreme God, El, and the other spirits that spoke to him resulted in such terrible tragedy.

A MESSAGE FROM MOSES

I. My Life on Earth

MOSES'S ACCOUNT OF THE EXODUS

I was born on the banks of the Nile River in Egypt to Hebrew parents who sent me downstream in a basket. As fortune would have it, I was eventually found by someone who raised me in the royal palace. My childhood was similar to that of Shakyamuni Buddha, and like him, I grew increasingly aware of the disparities between the lavish life of the palace and the lives of the oppressed people.

I always had a strong sense of justice. I believed that what is right is always right and that God's justice and righteousness should always prevail. I was eighteen when I learned about my birth parents. The news made me reflect; I asked myself whether God's justice and righteousness were being fulfilled in our land. I could not believe that God would permit such disparity to exist between the people of the palace and the people who were oppressed. I resolved that some day, I would take a stand and save my people. I waited patiently until the time was right, meanwhile devoting myself to education, reading, and the military arts.

When the day came, I began ministering to the oppressed people. I told them that their blood also flowed through my veins. I was one of them, even though fate had led me to grow up in the palace with royal status. I told them that we should ask the pharaoh to free them so they could have a chance to live in happiness and peace. As I went around, ministering to the people, my following gradually grew.

I spoke to the people in the palace and debated with them, risking making enemies as I challenged their comfortable assumptions. In the end, my opinion was not accepted. They were only human, and they did not want to let go of the slaves that they thought of as their possessions. I returned to the Hebrews and told them that Egypt belonged to the pharaoh, that his people had their own way of life, and that there was no need for us to destroy their lives for the sake of our happiness. Instead, we should leave Egypt and journey in search of our own land where we could plant our hopes. We could not create our utopia in Egypt, so this new land would become our own utopia. I told them that our land, the land of Canaan, was far from Egypt but would flow with milk and honey. The Hebrews began to dream of this new land.

Canaan really existed. My powerful spiritual abilities enabled me to see and experience it. I encouraged the Hebrews to believe in me. I told them that the land of Canaan, our Heaven, truly existed and that together, we would create a utopia there. It was imperative, I told them, that we act.

To help them believe in me and the things I was telling them, I used all my strength and all my spiritual abilities. I demonstrated my spiritual abilities at the palace, and I performed many miracles for the Hebrews, who saw them through spiritual eyes. Once, I released a staff from my hand and it transformed into a dragon that flew up into the sky. I was able to see the future and speak freely with holy spirits and with the god whom we knew at that time as Jehovah.

In time, I gathered hundreds of thousands of slaves from many regions and began the exodus from Egypt. The pharaoh's army pursued us, but we did not fight back; we just kept moving forward toward Canaan. Just as the Hebrew Bible describes, when we reached the Red Sea, I prayed to our god: "Heavens, break asunder! Earth, break asunder! Let us pass on our way to the land of Canaan. Jehovah, grant us your assistance. Grant us your assistance." That was what I prayed to Heaven, to the earth, and to our god.

That was when it happened. The Red Sea parted into two. There had never been such a miracle before. We quickly made our way through the dry path, and when the pharaoh's army pursued us, they were swallowed by the closing sea. That was how we were able to safely cross the Red Sea. The Red Sea was not a large body of water, but it was certainly a miracle that its waters parted. Our god had been planning a homeland for the people of Israel, and He created this path for them.*

THE TEN COMMANDMENTS

We successfully departed from Egypt and wandered for decades in search of Canaan. Many of us died from hunger on our journey. We were attacked, but we united and fought our attackers bravely. At one point, we reached a mountain. At the foot of this mountain I received a message from Yahweh, so I told my people to wait for me while I climbed the mountain. When I reached the top, I prayed to my god and received the Ten Commandments. He engraved them onto a slab of stone. He wrote: "You shall not kill. Honour thy father and thy mother. You shall not covet thy neighbour's goods."

When I took the stone tablet back to my people, none of them believed me. I was enraged to find that they were worshipping golden statues. I taught them not to worship such idols, and when I destroyed their statues, the stone tablet also crumbled into pieces. I went up the mountain once more and prayed to my god again.

---

* It was clearly an ethnic god who instructed Moses to lead an exodus out of Egypt to create the land of Israel, promised Moses the land of Canaan, and ordered Moses to kill the native people of his destination in order to create his own nation.

My god granted me the revelations again: "You shall have no other gods before me. Honour thy father and thy mother. You shall not kill. You shall not covet the goods of others." He gave me the Ten Commandments again, one after another.

I brought the new slab back to the people, showed them the Ten Commandments, and instructed them to obey these teachings. I must confess, however, that I also made mistakes. I heard not only the voice of my god, but also that of Satan. There were times when I mistook the voice of Satan for my god's voice. The voice of Satan said to me, "Moses, prayers alone will not please your god. You must also slaughter a lamb and dedicate the blood to him. Your god will be pleased by your sacrifice." But, of course, our true God would not be pleased by a bloody lamb, nor any sacrifice. What God desires is our pure mind, our righteous mind, our just mind. He would never want the blood of sacrificial lambs. But unfortunately, because of my error, sacrificial rituals became widespread. This was one of my teachings that was wrong.

We continued on our journey, but we never did reach the land of Canaan. I lived well over one hundred years and eventually passed away at the foot of a mountain. My life was devoted to leading my people and trying to build the nation of Israel. I gathered the Israelites to me and led them through many decades of wandering. I showed them many miracles and gave them the Ten Commandments. I became the first person to create a monotheistic religion. That was my life.

II. The Path of Righteousness

BE STRONG, FOR GOD IS STRONG

Justice is the focus of my role in Heaven. Justice means doing what is right, and doing what is right means following reason. The foundation of my philosophy is my belief that the righteous must be strong.

Those who are righteous need to be strong.
Those who live by God's teachings need to be strong.
Those who expound teachings about righteousness need to be
   strong.
Those who live with righteousness need to be strong.
Those who voice what is right need to be strong.
Those who convey the Truth as Truth need to be strong.

We need to live courageously. I would like the righteous to be much stronger. We must never become discouraged or fear opposition. We should never give in to fear, become daunted by obstacles, tremble in trepidation, or succumb to cowardice. Remember the strife and the hardships of your predecessors, and ask yourselves whether you have been living idly. I would like you to live with great courage. The more fortunate your circumstances, the more earnestly you should live out your lives. Remind yourselves of the hard battles that your predecessors fought and the difficult circumstances they faced. If you find yourself in more fortunate circumstances, then you have a duty to achieve greater heights. So be strong. I would like the righteous and those who have faith in God to be stronger. If you find weaknesses in yourself, then develop strength through self-reflection.

I can only speak to you abstractly. I will not tell you in detail what you should do. I would like you to have an unshakable mind. Do not be defeated by fears about what people might say to you. There is no need to provoke conflicts with the people around you, but do stay strong, for the righteous should always live with strength. I lived out my life with courage and strength. You need strength and passion to spread the Truths. If you believe that you are righteous, then you must use your willpower to live courageously.

Strength comes from God; it is a part of His essence. There

is nothing for us to fear, as long as we trust that God is on our side and supporting us. I cannot stress these things enough: the righteous need to be strong, and the world needs to accept truth as truth. We should never pander to wrong teachings or wrong actions. We should never compromise our opinions, even when we are confronted with many opinions that challenge or conflict with ours.

Many old religions exist, but we should never pander to the followers of old teachings. We will face much adversity and many difficulties and conflicts whenever we expound new teachings, and we must never give up. Since God is strong, we do not need to be afraid to state facts as facts and to describe right as right. A great God who can perform profound miracles is with us. So we must believe in the power of our great God, for our strong belief will make that power even stronger. God's power is as strong as our faith in Him. The more we believe and the stronger our faith becomes, the more God's glory and God's miracles will manifest.

It is foolish for human beings to try to measure God's mind, because it is impossible to gauge God's power based on human faculties of reason and intellect. One thousand days for us is like one day for God. An enormous army to us is just a line of marching ants to God. Mount Everest is nothing but a crease in his shirt. To God, the vast universe is just a corner of a miniature garden. This great God is watching over us and supporting us. We are all tiny ants living in His miniature garden. Our perception of the world is limited.

Sometimes we, these tiny ants, have trouble choosing which direction to go. A mound of sand can seem like a gigantic mountain. But God can destroy this mountain in an instant with one swipe of a hand and provide us with a panoramic view of our path forward. The difference between God and humans is even greater than the difference between ants and human beings. There is nothing in this world that God cannot do. Everything is possible for God. God's power is so great that He can create or destroy anything at His will. Creation and destruction are parts of God's essence.

A path will open for those who believe in God. Possibilities are opened to us based on how much we believe. If miracles are not happening in your life, the reason lies in weakness of faith. As long as your belief is strong, your mind will be ready to accept miracles. The door to your mind opens the moment you begin to believe. God's energy will pour into you depending on how wide your door has opened.

God's energy is limitless. It is a torrential river of unlimited energy. But no matter how much energy God sends us, it cannot reach us if our doors are closed. We need to open the doors to our mind to allow God's energy to fill us. We must begin, therefore, with faith.

Faith will give us the strength and ability to protect what is right. Different people have expressed righteousness in many different ways. As you learn different teachings, you will discover the diverse shapes that righteousness has taken. We should remember, however, that the essence of righteousness never changes, no matter how diverse its expressions are. What is right is expressed in many ways, but it always comes back to one source.

God sees our world as good. All the diverse expressions of righteousness can be summarized by this one ultimate truth: He believes our world is good. This ultimate truth has been expressed through Shakyamuni Buddha's teachings, Jesus's teachings, through philosophy and art, and in many other ways. Therefore, we must try to discover the unchanging truth within the various shapes and forms that righteousness has taken. God sees everything as good; He wishes to help all this goodness shine forth. Everything is good in its essence, and God wants to help everything be good in its manifestation. Everyone is good in essence, and God wants to help everyone do good work in this world.

PRESERVING THE TRUTHS FOR FUTURE GENERATIONS

Everyone living today has a mission to pass down the Truths for a thousand or even two thousand years. Times change, and circumstances change. But everything that changes is just part of the times. These changes are not significant. No matter what changes—even if dinosaurs suddenly begin to live around us or if we are suddenly surrounded by robots—our teachings about the mind will always be the same. Throughout history, we have always taught the importance of having a right mind that follows God's mind, and this teaching applies to the modern age, too. The mind is everything; we must follow the right law that will unite our minds with God. We must keep teaching about God's mind.

The modern age is filled with religious conflicts because many people cannot comprehend the original teachings of the founders of their traditional religions. But the conflicts between religions are not a result of the original teachings; rather, they occur because there is an absence of teaching.

Some of the people you encounter will comprehend the Truths, and others will not. Regardless of how many people understand the Truths, you must preserve the teachings for later generations.

We cannot blame the teacher when a student does not get a perfect score on an exam. Even when teachers do their best and teach students as well as they can, some students will score 30 percent and others will score 70 percent. Based on your standards, the former students will have failed. But this will have happened not because of the teachings but because the students were not able to understand what they were being taught.

Sometimes people do not understand the teachings because their minds are being influenced by Devils. Devils were not created as Devils; they are simply people who are not living in accord with

God's mind. Because of their wrong state of mind, Devils confuse other people and obstruct our work. The mind that allows them to hinder our progress is a wrong state of mind.

It is extremely rare for people like me to appear on Earth— we appear only during turning points in history or in times of great upheaval. It is also very rare for us to speak through some-one who is living, as I am doing right now. Therefore, when you are given the opportunity to leave behind the highest teachings, it is very important that you do so. Even I cannot be sure how many people will believe in these words I speak today. Regard-less, it is imperative that you make the effort to leave behind our teachings.

WE ARE EQUAL FRAGMENTS OF GOD WITH DIFFERENT INTENSITIES OF LIGHT

The spirit world is divided into different levels, but the idea that a hierarchy exists can be dangerous if it is taken to an extreme. We must not allow this idea to lead to discrimination. We should always adopt a balanced way of thinking that unites our perception of difference with our commitment to equality. It is important to stress that all human souls are equal. To see some people as superior and others as inferior is one way of perceiving. At the same time, everyone is a child of God, and we are equal in that all of us were given souls.

Each of our souls was originally a part of God. We are frag-ments of God. God's essence is also our essence. In the beginning, we were all given equally precious souls, and our souls then gained spiritual training over the course of countless reincarnations. Over an immeasurable length of time, our souls developed different in-tensities of light. Some souls developed a wonderful radiance; others developed a dull sheen; and still others have not developed any light. Everyone is equal, but the process of reincarnation has given us different amounts of light.

When we speak of bodhisattvas or angels and of *tathagatas* or great angels, and when we say that a soul is from the World of Goodness, we are simply describing these various grades of light. But this doesn't mean that there is any difference in the substance of the souls. Every soul has the potential to become a bodhisattva, or angel, and a *tathagata*, or great angel, if that soul experiences the right spiritual training. So even though our souls are equal, we can describe ourselves in terms of the differences in the intensity of the light that our souls radiate.

We can also describe ourselves in terms of the spiritual work for which we are responsible. Different people have developed different elements of their souls. For example, the ability to fulfill God's mission is especially developed in me, while other people have chosen to develop a different facet of their souls. Our different responsibilities are all important, so although we have developed our souls in different ways, our souls are still equal.

Different souls have achieved different heights, but there is no true ranking; the eighth dimension is not necessarily superior to the seventh dimension. Instead, I would like everyone to think of people as standing on the surface of a globe with God sitting at the North Pole. While there are times when the regions near the North Pole are advanced, there are also times when regions further away from the North Pole become advanced. And those whose light shines radiantly right now may become dulled down later, while those whose light is completely clouded right now may shine brightly later on. So I hope that everyone will try to see both difference and equality in the world.

III. Sin and Evil

THE NATURE OF SIN

Sins were not given to us by God. Sin and evil are created when the light inside us as children of God is replaced by something foreign. The true purpose of everyone's body is to be a temple of God where the Holy Spirit resides and tries to fulfil its duties. God is at work in our bodies, conveying His will and fulfilling His objectives. At our best, we hear God's voice within us and set to work on God's tasks. But sometimes, we do not hear God's voice, or we do not listen, or we disregard it. We commit sins, create evil, and become lost in delusions; we pursue different objectives and behave in ways that defile our nature as children of God.

Evil was never an independent existence; it came about when we began to sell things in our sacred temple. If you ever tried to sell goods in a real temple, the astonished priests would immediately ask you to leave. That is what sin is: doing things that you are not supposed to do inside your holy temple, which is meant to be a place of faith, prayer, and communion with God.

Nature has endowed us with the gift of intelligence, but sometimes we misuse this gift. For example, we should never sell fish or fruit in the temple. Conducting business is not evil in itself, but it is wrong to do it in a temple. There is a delusion in choosing an inappropriate time, location, and method. We should stop our five senses from creating delusions and leading us to give in to temptation. It is wrong and a sin to do something in a temple that should not be done there, and it is wrong and a sin to bring something to a temple that does not belong there.

Sometimes, the temple priest may try to teach us about the holiness of the temple by hanging signs forbidding the sale of goods inside it. Some merchants will obey the signs, understanding that the temple is a sacred ground and not a place to do business. But other merchants will not notice the signs and will begin selling their products anyway. Still others will see the signs but will not understand what they mean. And yet others will disregard the signs and argue that doing business where many people gather is a great way to make a profit and so we should be allowed to do business wherever we like. This is an evil, a sin.

The priest in this story is an apostle of light. Age after age, apostles of light come down to Earth to guide people to the path of goodness. The merchants in this story are the people who do not listen to these apostles, instead ignoring them and setting up their businesses inside holy temples. The signs that the priest sets up are the sutras in Buddhism and the Bible in Christianity. The Bible teaches what people should and should not do and how people should do things, but many people who read it choose not to follow it. Others see the Bible or the Buddhist sutras but choose not to read them at all. They are still people like us, and they are good citizens if they are doing their businesses in appropriate places. They have children to feed and lives to fend for. It is just wrong to do business in a temple, since the temple is not meant for that purpose.

Mistakes committed unknowingly are more serious than those committed knowingly. For example, some people commit murder even though they know that it is wrong and a punishable crime. Others kill without hesitation simply because they want to, not even knowing whether it is right or wrong and without giving a thought to whether it is good or evil. Which of these people are further away from God and more dangerous to society?

Sometimes, we face unavoidable circumstances that lead us to commit sins. It is a graver sin to commit wrongs without knowing that they are wrongs. Knowledge of what is right and wrong is bound to awaken one's conscience, hesitation, and remorse, at least. The killer who knows that killing is a sin will be in agony as his good conscience and evil mind are pitted against each other. But those who do not know that what they do is a sin will not experience this pang of conscience.

WHY GOD ALLOWS EVIL TO EXIST

There is a reason why God allows evil to exist. Imagine a priest giving a sermon at a Sunday service to many pious men and women. Suddenly, a group of intruders barges into the church. If you were the priest, what would you do? In front of you is an audience of three hundred good men, women, and children, who are earnestly listening to your sermon about the Holy Bible. But the intruders ridicule your words. They shout that there is no God and that the Bible is useless because it does not help people get rich. There are more fun things to do on Sundays than go to church, they say.

As the priest, you could make any number of choices in this situation. You could call the police and have them forcibly remove the intruders from the church. You could surround the intruders and beat them on the grounds that people like them should not even exist. You could leave them alone and allow them to keep disrupting your sermon. But the best thing you could do is appeal to the intruders' consciences. If you allow your mind to become consumed by hatred and choose to get rid of the intruders, your mind will no longer be with God. Your mind will be in the hands of the Devil.

Situations like this are conflicts between the Devil and the Holy Spirit. The priest represents the Holy Spirit. If you, as the priest, make the effort to lead the intruders to faith by appealing to their consciences, then you will not lose the respect of your church members. A true and faithful servant of God would be as compassionate as possible and would do all that he or she could to talk to the intruders.

Many people wonder why the Devil still exists even after thousands years of our teachings. They also wonder why Hell has not disappeared after all this time. This is because we are using the most inefficient method of ridding the world of evil. The most efficient thing to do would be to get rid of these agitators by force and make them vanish. But we choose to use a method that takes more time and patience: speaking to their consciences and waiting for them to awaken. We continue to devote our lives to expounding God's laws, regardless of Satan.

In the end, people commit sins because of a lack of knowledge. If the Devil and his people knew about Heaven, they would not be in Hell. They have forgotten the joy of being in Heaven and having light. They believe that their world is the truth. They see the faithful as devils trying to destroy their world. They can only think about themselves and try to protect their interests, status, and security. And it is always difficult to determine whether or not they are committing sins with an awareness of their self-centeredness.

IV. A New Age of Justice

OUR WORLD NEEDS JUSTICE

I believe that three things are indispensable: love, justice, and compassion. We need to actualize righteousness in this world. Justice is God's Truths. We need justice to give us the strength to dispel the forces that are not God's Truths so we can actualize God's Truths in our world and build a kingdom of God.

Justice is the strength that creates the foundation of our house of God. Love is the nails, the cement, and the clay that binds together timber and stone. Love is the bond that adheres us together in creating a kingdom of God.

In today's age, justice is long forgotten. Many of our religions lack justice. But I believe that God's laws need to be kept strong. We must defend justice, even if it means risking religious wars and persecution by adherents of other religions.

For thousands of years, the Ten Commandments have served as a valuable code of conduct. Now, in this age of confusion, we need a new form of the Ten Commandments. We need new guidelines about the right values and the principles of conduct that are suited to today's people. Religion is not simply about believing in spirits or making friends with one another. Religion is about following God's guidelines to create a foundation for a new civilization and culture. It is the mission of those living today to leave behind this gift for humankind.

You must look into the future. Do not think about what you are facing right now. Instead, think about the messages you want to leave behind for those who will be here two thousand and three thousand years from now. My name and my words may not survive that long. By then, both Jesus Christ and I may be thought of as mythical figures. But the teachings you convey must survive and be known as historical truth.

In the final analysis, the future depends on your explaining clearly why God created this world and why God designed the world to help us reincarnate through Heaven. You must explain the underlying principles, and you must explain how we should live out our lives. Future generations require nothing more and nothing less.

A NEW AGE IS DAWNING

I have spoken a great deal today about civilization and culture, and the reason is that a new age is dawning as we speak. The sun of the Truths is rising, and people need to realize that a new era is in the making.

I would like everyone to know why Moses has awakened from three thousand years of silence to give this message to the people on Earth. I have provided inspiration to many people during that time, but never before, since the time of my death, have my thoughts been conveyed in my own words. This is the first time I have ever provided guidance to people on Earth in this form.

This great miracle is deeply significant. This ultimate miracle marks the arrival of the new age. Healing, materialization of physical objects, and predictions of the future are not the greatest miracles. The greatest miracle possible is expounding God's mind directly, exactly as God speaks it. This is nearly impossible, but we come infinitely close when those nearest God convey God's mind on God's behalf.

Those of you who observe this miracle must open your spiritual eyes and experience the awesomeness. It is no ordinary occurrence. You must realize that Moses has awakened from three thousand years of silence to split the physical world with his message as I once split the Red Sea. I am trying to split in half the miniature garden you live in that is isolated from the spirit world. This miracle is happening right now.

Incredible things are happening around you. A gospel is being given in your presence. Please understand the significance of this event, experience the awe, understand the value of this time, and appreciate how precious it is to be living when this miracle is happening. There is no time to waste. You should feel the most passionate desire to experience this miracle with your own eyes, no matter how long the journey will take by air, sea, or land. If you are truly seeking the ultimate way of life, this desire should consume you.

A miracle that occurs only once every several thousand years is happening right now. The enormous sun of the Truths is rising. Watch this sun, see its tremendous size, see its enormous light, and see its incredible power.

AUTHOR'S THOUGHTS

THE PROHIBITION OF IDOLATRY

Moses lived about 3,200 years ago. The ancestors of the Israelites originally lived in the desert and later moved to Egypt, where they were taken captive and had to work as slaves. So Moses led the Israelites out of Egypt and back to their homeland in the desert. The Hebrew Bible describes this historical event.

According to the Bible, Moses spent forty days in the mountains. The Israelites used the number "forty" to mean "many," so we do not need to take this number literally. While in the mountains, Moses received revelations from God in the form of the Ten Commandments. I am not sure whether it is true that God engraved the Ten Commandments on the two stone tablets, but it is true that Moses returned from the mountain with them.

While Moses was meditating in the mountains, Aaron and the other Israelites wanted something they could worship, so they created a statue of a golden calf by melting down and reshaping their gold earrings and accessories. When Moses came down from the mountain, he saw Aaron and the rest of the people dancing, singing, and worshiping this statue.

Unfortunately, Moses was so outraged by this that in a fit of anger, he threw the stone tablets, breaking them into pieces. He was angry because the Israelites' conduct was breaking Yahweh's first commandment, which prohibited the worship of idols: "You shall have no other gods before me. You shall not make for yourself an idol, whether in the form of anything that is in heaven above, or that is on the earth beneath, or that is in the water under the earth" (Deut. 5:7-5:8). Yahweh was extremely angered by this conduct.

To this day, people believe this prohibition of idol worship to be the word of God. But it was actually Yahweh who created this commandment. There was a reason Yahweh disliked idol worship: the Egyptians, who had enslaved the Israelites, created many statues of their gods. Many of them can still be seen in Egyptian temples and buildings. Yahweh disliked the Egyptians and did not want the Israelites to perpetuate Egyptian culture.

From a broader perspective, idol worship existed in many other parts of the world in regions such as ancient Greece and India. These regions developed a culture of representing their gods through statues. We can visit Greece today and still see many marble statues of the Greek gods. And in India, some of Shakyamuni Buddha's followers created statues of him while he was alive, and many more statues of him were created after his death. In comparison, the desert regions developed a culture of prohibiting statues of gods and even promoted iconoclasm, the destruction of religious statues.

THE ANCIENT CIVILIZATIONS AND THEIR COMPETING GODS

The civilizations of Greece, India, and Egypt can be traced back to Hermes, Shakyamuni Buddha, and Thoth and Hermes, respectively. Moses's account of Egyptian history creates a lot of confusion, but the truth is that the Thoth-Hermes philosophy had existed in Egypt since ancient times. When I explained history from Moses's perspective, it was difficult for me to reveal these details. The Thoth faith spread to Egypt from Atlantis, where Thoth was worshiped as the god of their civilization, and Hermes began to guide Egypt when he finished guiding Greece. El Cantare focused his guidance on Greece, Rome, and Egypt for a long time, and these areas developed cultures in which statues of gods were seen as good things.

When Moses left Egypt to lead the Exodus, Egypt was at its peak of civilization; it was the strongest country in the world. It followed that the Egyptian religion was also very strong and widespread. The Egyptian gods were very powerful and influential and were backed by thousands of years of history. There was an extremely strong spiritual culture that had been developed by Hermes Trismegistus, whom we also call El Cantare.

Moses and his people were a minority group in Egypt. The god that Moses believed in was a minor god of slaves who wanted to deny the god of Egypt and Greece. This was why Moses's god proclaimed that his people should not believe in any other god but himself and prohibited the worship of statues. This was the start of the religious conflicts we have seen throughout history.

El Cantare did not completely ignore the Middle Eastern regions, however. A belief in the God El has existed in the Middle Eastern world since ancient times. El was also known as Elohim, and Elohim was the God of love, El Cantare. The history of the Israelites is filled with prophets. It would be easy to assume that all these prophets believed in Yahweh, since Yahweh had said that his followers must not worship any other god. But not all the prophets were under Yahweh's guidance; some of them were receiving guidance from El Cantare.

In ancient times, faith in El spread very widely throughout the desert regions. But this faith was interrupted by the emergence of monotheism and the prohibition of idol worship. This trend lasted for one thousand years, beginning with Judaism and continuing to some degree in Christianity. As we can see by the Catholic Church's veneration of statues of Mary and Jesus, Christianity does not completely follow the commandment against idolatry. But we see that commandment against idolatry has influenced Christianity to some degree because Greek Orthodox believers, who pray fervently in front of paintings, insist that they are not practicing idolatry because paintings are not statues. Islam is another monotheistic religion that forbids idol worship. All three religions—Judaism, Christianity, and Islam—have at least traces of the prohibition of idol worship that Yahweh developed in opposition to El.

YAHWEH, MONOTHEISM, AND RELIGIOUS CONFLICT

Monotheistic religions have a problem: their scriptures describe more than one god. It is the real nature of the spirit world that many gods exist and that some gods are stronger and on a higher level than others. The ancient Greek and Egyptian religions were polytheistic, and Buddhists believe that there have been many buddhas throughout history. Polytheism has been the mainstream theology of the world. This tradition was disrupted when Yahweh appeared and declared that he was the one and only god.

Yahweh told Moses that he would grant him the land of Canaan, so Moses set out from Egypt toward that region. But Canaan was already inhabited by indigenous Arabs. The Arabs were outraged by this god who wanted to take their land. The Hebrews may have argued that they should take over the land because their god had commanded it. But the Arabs would naturally argue that their god had never said such a thing.

This was the beginning of a long history of religious conflict that has continued for thousands of years. The religious conflicts between Israel and the Arab countries can be traced back to Moses's time, when there was a territorial conflict between different gods. It is a sad truth, but some gods do not like to cooperate.

Another problem is found in Yahweh's sixth commandment: thou shalt not kill. The Hebrew Bible says that when Moses returned from the mountain and found Aaron and the Hebrews worshiping a statue of a golden calf, he ordered three thousand Hebrews to be killed. This is a shocking story on its own, but in addition, it creates many problems to believe in a god who teaches not to kill but who then orders the deaths of three thousand people because they have not followed his teachings. In the end, Yahweh was saying that anyone who has faith in him should not be killed.

Religious conflicts boil down to two points: religions' different stances toward idol worship and their different concepts of sacrificial offering—in other words, the idea of killing people for the sake of God. Heaven has not completely accepted one stance or the other. We should be aware, however, that a foreign way of thinking has infiltrated the mainstream teachings and that the confusion between Yahweh and Elohim is the source of the conflicts in the Middle East.

CHAPTER 4

MUHAMMAD

Be Humble before God

THE LIFE OF MUHAMMAD

Muhammad was born in 570 CE, almost 540 years after the death of Jesus Christ, in Mecca, which was a trading center in western Arabia. He was born into the Banu Hashim, a branch of the powerful Quraysh tribe that dominated Mecca. Muhammad had a very difficult childhood. His father, Abd Allah, died before Muhammad was born, and his mother, Aminah, passed away when he was only six years old, leaving him an orphan. He then went to live with his grandfather, Abd al-Muttalib, who also died, two years later. Finally, Muhammad was taken in by his father's brother, Abu Talib.

At age twenty-five, Muhammad married Khadijah, a beautiful and affluent forty-year-old widow who owned a trade caravan. The couple was blessed with three sons and four daughters. Muhammad spent the first fifteen years of his marriage living the life of a wealthy merchant—but fate had another plan in store for him.

It was Muhammad's practice to spend a certain part of the year meditating and praying in a cave in the mountains approximately five kilometers (three miles) northeast of Mecca. One night in the year 610, when he was forty years old, he had an overpowering spiritual experience in a cave on Mt. Hira during the month of Ramadan. A solemn voice rang out through the cave, and a luminous being grasped him by the throat and told him to remember and recite the words of God that would be revealed to him and to make a record of them later.

Muhammad was terrified; he thought that he was being possessed by the jinn—the demon of the desert—and tried to avoid his fate. However, encouraged by his wife Khadijah, he gradually came to accept his calling, and around 613, he began to preach his messages to the people. Khadijah was very supportive of Muhammad and became his first convert. Ultimately, after talking with several Jews and with Khadijah's cousin, Waraqa, who was a Christian, Muhammad came to believe that the being who had been speaking to him since the "Night of Power" had been Jibril, the archangel Gabriel.

Muhammad passed on numerous revelations to his people. His revelations were written down during the reign of the third caliph, Uthman, who promulgated an official version of the Koran that consisted of 114 chapters. Muhammad taught a monotheistic faith in Allah as the sole God, and his teachings can be summed up under the following themes: angels, scriptures, prophets, life after death, and predestination.

Muhammad had been strongly influenced by the Jews and Christians he had met during his travels in Syria as a merchant, and this led him to deny the idolatry of Meccans who worshipped the sun, stars, and rocks. His new religion spread like wildfire, finding eager supporters among slaves and the poor. But the ruling Quraysh tribe of his birth persecuted him, so in 622, he escaped from Mecca and migrated to Medina. This event, known to Muslims as the Hijrah, marks the first year of the Muslim calendar. In Medina, Muhammad organized his religious order and built an army, and in 630, he marched into Mecca and conquered it with the intention of unifying Arabia.

Muhammad was originally from the world of tathagatas in the eighth dimension of Heaven. The messages he received in the cave originated from the same group of divine spirits who had guided Jesus and the Hebrew prophets. But two things made Muhammad different: first, he preached in the midst of a merchant economy, and second, he commanded a powerful military force. Muhammad's political and military power led him to stress the importance of the jihad, the holy war, which became the foundation for the strife among Muslims that continues to this day. Even in the present day, the Middle East remains covered by a thick fog of negative thoughts.

Also, because the Koran focused on precepts and teachings about worship and fasting, Islam eventually got too caught up in rules and forms and began to lose its teachings about the mind. Unlike Jesus, Muhammad never had a chance to undergo extensive religious training, so he was unable to deepen his understanding of the revelations that he had received and to develop them into spiritual teachings.

One of the most distinctive features of Muhammad's teachings was their regard for Allah as the one and only God; previously, Meccans had revered Allah as the Supreme God, the highest god among many other gods. Based on my investigations and research into the spirit world, their understanding was right: many divine spirits exist in the spirit world. But Muhammad focused only on Allah, saying that Allah was the sole God. Muhammad denied the Quraysh's understanding that Allah was the highest god among the divinities and spoke as if all the other gods were evil spirits. This triggered war between Muhammad and the Quraysh. Muhammad was not fighting against the Devil; he was fighting over ideological conflicts. The war was caused by Muhammad's limited understanding and lack of higher awareness.

After the death of Khadijah, Muhammad took more than ten new wives, including his favorite, Aisha. This practice of polygamy led some Christians to consider Islam an evil religion, but there was a practical reason that polygamy was endorsed: it provided a type of basic social security to the many Muslims who were orphaned and widowed as a result of the region's recurrent religious wars. It is also important to note that the rules of Islam required husbands to treat each wife equally.

A MESSAGE FROM MUHAMMAD

ISLAM IS A TOLERANT RELIGION

I was born in Mecca, in what is now Saudi Arabia. Mecca's ruling tribe at the time, the Quraysh, practiced polytheism. When I was forty, I went to the cave known as Hira to meditate and fast. While meditating, I received divine revelations that led me to spread a monotheistic religion. Historically, polytheism had been dominant, not only in Mecca, but also in ancient Greece, Egypt, and the rest of Africa. Monotheism only began to spread in that region when Christianity emerged.

I taught monotheism in an area that was predominantly polytheistic; I said that Allah was the sole God and that His teachings were the only correct teachings. Because of this teaching, I was persecuted by the Quraysh and forced to flee Mecca. So I moved to Medina and from there waged a fairly long battle against the Quraysh tribe in Mecca. Life in Medina was very difficult and dangerous, but because I was blessed with military talent, I won the final battle and returned to Mecca triumphant. Islamic teachings spread because my military victory enabled me to unify the people politically. To create a unified, national religion, I needed to integrate the religion with the military and political life of the nation. This is the history surrounding the founding of Islam.

You may see Islam as an aggressive religion because of its founding history, but the word "Islam" means "peace." We are people who hope for peace. Most Christians today misunderstand us. Over the course of history, Christians launched many crusades against Islam to reclaim Jerusalem, Christianity's holy land. But Jerusalem was also a holy land for Islam, so we fought many battles over the city. Because of this, Christians came to regard us as confrontational foes.

During my time, Islam accepted other philosophies and religions, including our forerunner, Christianity. We even accepted the ancient Jewish prophets. We were very tolerant. Despite our tolerance, Christians saw Islam as a false religion and persecuted us. Christians have a history of persecution among themselves, as well. After the death of Jesus Christ, many Christians were persecuted by other Christians as heretics and were burned at the stake. Angels of Light were killed at the hands of their own people.

Although Islamic teachings were tolerant, we had to transform ourselves. If we had remained tolerant when we had an intolerant opponent launching fierce attacks against us, we would have been easily defeated. Even if you have accepted the other party, you can't put up with them attacking you and invading you, claiming that you are promulgating teachings of Satan. This is indeed a difficult matter. In most cases, those that come afterward either tolerate those that came before them or completely reject them.

I think what annoys Christians is actually the tolerant aspect of Islam. They would rather we deny Jesus completely so that it would be clear that we want a total war with them. But we recognize Jesus as a prophet—one of the many prophets of the Old Testament. For me, the idea that the Creator God had an "only Son" meant that He had a wife and a family, which was blaspheming God. So I said that that was impossible and that when Jesus was described as God's "only Son," it simply meant that he was a human being. But I guess my halfhearted and vague way of putting things provoked their wrath even more.

I think we were tolerant, because we recognized Christianity. At least, I myself acknowledged Christianity, and I said that Christians could remain Christians. We didn't accuse them of heresy or kill them for belonging to a different religion. I think that Christians and Jews killed more heretics than we Muslims did. They were more violent; they went so far as to burn people at the stake.

All I asked was that Christians pay a tax. If they paid a tax, they could remain Christians. If they converted to Islam, they would be exempt from this tax. I guess what I did was more like pork-barrel politics, in modern terms, but this is something you all would do, right? I mean, if you tell people they can either stay with their current faith and pay a tax or convert and not pay the tax, they'll be motivated to convert. I was just good with this kind of maneuvering because I was from the merchant class. But we didn't go so far as to deny their faith. In any case, we were accepting and tolerant of Christianity, so we see Islam as a peaceful and tolerant religion. So, please do not be afraid of Muslims. Muslims are taught to love peace. Islam teaches mercy and peace. I hope that you understand this.

WINNING A MILITARY VICTORY

There is no mention of suicide bombing in Islamic teachings. There is only the idea of the jihad, the holy war fought to defend the teachings of Islam. People today may see Islam as an aggressive, bloodthirsty, and narrow-minded religion, since Muslims tend not to be afraid of war and conflict. But this is because, while I was a religious leader who conveyed God's words, I was also a military hero. Muslims worship military heroes.

Similarly, there were many war gods in Japanese Shintoism. In the process of building a nation, there is always a battle with the former regime. Those who have fought, won, and brought peace to their nation become gods. So it is only natural for people to worship as war gods the military heroes that built their nation. This was actually the reason Christianity didn't spread in Japan. Because Japanese people worshiped war gods, they just couldn't accept the Christian teaching that the son of the omnipotent God had been so easily captured and crucified by his enemies.

When we moved from Mecca to Medina, we set up lines of resistance against the Meccan army. The Meccans probably saw my teachings as the teachings of the Devil, so they marched on Medina with their army. They outnumbered us—their army was ten times the size of ours—but we were able to defeat them because I invented trench warfare for the first time in history. It was actually Hermes who spiritually guided me to come up with the idea of trench warfare. He taught me, through inspiration, that we could avoid getting hit by their arrows if we dug a hole and attacked from there. I had archery units attack from trenches. I also invented rank formation and had archers fire in turn. I believe that Oda Nobunaga of Japan came up with the same tactic about a thousand years later, in the latter half of the sixteenth century. He defeated the powerful Takeda cavalry by lining his rifle battalion up in three lines that fired in turn. This was the same technique I had used a thousand years earlier. It took time for archers to reset their bows after shooting an arrow. So I lined them up in two or three rows and had them fire in turn. This allowed the battalion to continuously fire arrows and saved time. By reducing the time it took to nock an arrow, we were able to fire three times faster than our enemy. In modern terms, it was like using machine guns against rifles. It was because we invented this continuous shooting tactic and trench warfare that our Medinan army was able to defeat the Meccan army.

With this victory, our forces grew. We attracted allies because they saw our victory as a miracle, and eventually we were able to occupy Mecca and build a new nation. Muslims believe that I, Muhammad, am greater than Jesus because I was also a military hero who built a nation.

According to Jewish tradition, the Messiah had to be a political leader and a hero that saved his country. The Jews of Israel did not accept Jesus as the Messiah because he was crucified. For Jews, a Messiah was supposed to be someone like King David. Jesus did not satisfy the criteria for the Messiah as set forth in the Hebrew Bible. From a Jewish perspective, I actually qualify to be the Messiah, because I fought, won, and saved my country.

Muslims do not deny Jesus; we recognize him as a great man and a prophet. We do not see Jesus as the Messiah, however, because that would make Islam a denomination of Christianity. We see Jesus as one of the many prophets of ancient Israel. I think that Jesus was born as a prophet with a mission to become the Messiah, but unfortunately, he did not succeed at spreading his teachings while he was alive and was crucified in the end. From a worldly perspective, he failed, so I thought that it was appropriate to regard Jesus as a prophet.

Many prophets have been persecuted as Jesus was. But I fought, won, and built the nation of Islam. I established Islam as the national religion and unified politics, the military, and religion. Our teachings did not glorify the leader of a losing battle—they glorified the winning leader. Islam fulfilled its mission, in that sense, and it became a world religion. This is why Muslims think that Muhammad is greater than Jesus.

RECEIVING REVELATIONS FROM HEAVEN
Muslims also call me "the last prophet" because of my superiority in another respect: Islam is based on spiritual revelations—words

of God—that were conveyed through me while I was alive. This is the basis of the Koran. This is what makes Islam superior to Christianity, in my opinion.

Allah is the god of Islam, but the word "Allah" simply means "God." When we say "Allah," we are referring to the Creator God. Christians have criticized me, saying that there was no way that the Creator would speak directly through my mouth. But if you look at the Old Testament, many prophets heard the words of God. God spoke to Noah, Abraham, and others just as a human being would speak to another human being. So just as the Creator God spoke to the Jewish prophets, He spoke to me. I had the ability to hear the voice of God.

The ancient Hebrew prophets heard and received the words of God, but they couldn't convey the teachings of God directly to the people in the form of spiritual revelations. Neither the ancient prophets nor Jesus could do this. Only I was able to directly receive and deliver the teachings of God, and these teachings have been passed down in the holy book, the Koran. Christians were never able to produce a scripture that contained the words of God as completely as the Koran did. The Christian Bible contains fragments of Jesus's words; otherwise, it is a historical record of his deeds and conversations with his disciples. Because the Koran was a compilation of God's words, we believe that Islam is a more complete religion than Christianity.

The basic teachings of Islam are based on Christianity. They are based on the Old and New Testaments. We accept Christian beliefs. The Christian god is the same god that Muslims worship. But Christians have fiercely criticized us, saying that their god is different from our god. They have also criticized us because I founded a religion based on spiritual revelations that I received from God. Christianity is different in that it is based on the record of Jesus's words and deeds. So it is not based on direct revelations from Heaven.

Christians argued that God would not send His words directly through a human being. So after studying with my Christian acquaintances, I changed how I talked about my revelation. I still believed that I had directly received the words of God, but some of my Christian acquaintances told me that people might think I was arrogant and irreverent for saying that. They suggested that I compromise on that point so that we could reconcile with Christians. It was true that I heard a number of different voices, so I suppose multiple spirits were guiding me at that time. Actually, there were at least forty different spirits that used the name "Allah" when they sent me messages. So a team of guiding spirits worked together to form the teachings of Islam. The voices of Allah that I heard revealed the different ideas of many guiding spirits. That is why there are different writing styles in the Koran.

So I didn't change my stance that I was delivering the teachings of Allah, but I did change how I spoke about receiving them. In Christian teachings, Archangel Gabriel, who is one of the seven archangels, serves as God's messenger. In Islam, we call Gabriel by the name "Jibril." So I said that I had received God's words through Jibril. I thought that Christians would accept this interpretation of my experience. Our intention was to conciliate the Christians, not to persecute them. But now, I feel that we are in a dangerous situation in terms of our relations with the Christian world. Originally, we were sister religions, but those who are too close tend to despise each other.

Christianity was founded six hundred years before Islam, and since we were newer, we believed that we were more advanced. In fact, during the Middle Ages, Islam made great scientific advancements, while Christianity entered the Dark Ages. They held witch trials, burned heretics at the stake, and engaged in other brutal acts during that age. Meanwhile, Islam progressed and flourished. We became prosperous and advanced in the sciences, so it was only natural for us to think that Christianity would decline and that Islam would spread around the world. But Christianity regained some ground with the emergence of Martin Luther and John Calvin. Now, Islam and Christianity are in conflict over which religion is superior.

We believed that the teachings of Islam were connected to the teachings of the Old Testament and the New Testament and that we were sister religions. But the Christians disagreed and criticized us. They said that it was absurd to think that God would talk to me directly and that it was unacceptable to call Jesus a prophet. They also said that the words and parables of the Bible were superior to and more beautiful than those in the Koran. Christians claimed that the god of Christianity and the god of Islam must be different, because the parables and passages in the Koran were not aesthetic or pleasing as the ones in the Bible. In particular, the Koran includes many parables that use spiders and insects and other worldly creatures as metaphors. So they criticized us, saying that our parables lacked literary elegance and were not as poetic as those taught by Jesus. Thus, they claimed that we believed in a different god from theirs.

In addition to the Koran, Muslims have another scripture called the Hadith, which is a record of my words and deeds. It is a compilation of what I did and said and the decisions I made at different points in my life. The Hadith serves as a guidebook for my disciples and those in later generations to refer to when they do not know what to do in situations that are not specifically mentioned in the Koran. Muslims build their faith on these two pillars: the Koran and the Hadith. This is another reason that Muslims have believed that they are more advanced than Christians.

I also think Islam is superior to Christianity because it offers a clear perspective of the spirit world. Islam offers clear explanations about the spirit world, including both Heaven and Hell, which Christianity does not. Since Muslims believe in spiritual revelations, they have to believe in a spirit world. So I would say that Muslims are more spiritual.

Some early Christian sects were dedicated to mysticism and spiritualism, but other Christians persecuted these sects. For example, the Gnostic movement was guided by Hermes. Christianity lacked teachings about reincarnation and the spirit world, so to bring about a reformation of Christianity, Hermes sent angels of light who founded sects such as the Gnostics and the Cathari. But most of their members were killed. They were not just killed, but persecuted, slaughtered, and annihilated. This is what is terrifying about Christianity. Sufism, or the beliefs and practices of Islamic mysticism, was also guided mostly by Hermes and Thoth. Islam was largely divided into the Shia and Sunni sects, and it was the Sunnis that adopted Sufism widely. To completely deny Islam is to reject the teachings of Hermes.

MIRACLES AND GOD'S LOVE FOR MUHAMMAD

The fact that I was able to receive direct revelations and convey the word of the only God in the form of the Koran shows that my spiritual ability was superior to that of Jesus in some respects. This probably makes sense not only to Muslims, but also to non-Muslims. Jesus did not deliver the words of God as clearly as I did. He only went so far as to say that the words he spoke contained God's will. The spiritual messages that I conveyed prove my spiritual power. I also had an out-of-body experience, as described in the anecdote of my ascension to Heaven from Jerusalem. I guess you are only given the spiritual powers you need to fulfill your mission.

According to the Bible, Jesus cured illnesses and worked miracles, and his disciples also gained the ability to cure illnesses. Since then, however, only a few among popes and priests have been able to do this, and others with this ability were tried for heresy and burned at the stake. Surely, humans can be very jealous. Consequently, it seems as though miracles stopped occurring after the time of Jesus. I believe that Jesus's miracles prove that he was a Son of God. But miracles do not occur all the time, and it cannot be proved scientifically that they were real.

Miracles were also at work in my life; they included my divine revelations, my night journey, my miraculous victory in battle in spite of my overwhelmingly disadvantageous position, and the unification of the nation within my lifetime. I received my first revelations around the year 610 CE. Then, around the year 620 [622 CE], we fled from Mecca to Medina in what is called the Hijrah. After numerous battles, I attacked Mecca and won victory. Since we were at an overwhelming disadvantage, it surely was a miracle that we defeated the Meccan army and unified the country within ten years [in 630 CE].

I am sure that Christians wished that this kind of miracle had happened to Jesus, too. They probably wished that Jesus had received overwhelming support from the people when he made his entry to Jerusalem so that even the Roman soldiers would stop trying to capture him and would instead become his disciples. That way, Jerusalem would have become the kingdom of Jesus. Christians like to talk about establishing Jesus's kingdom, so that's probably what they wanted to happen. But it did not happen. Some may suspect that it was because God was not strong enough, but I think that God's love for me was stronger than His love for Jesus. God loved me and granted me victory.

Winning a war means that while people on one side survive,

those on the other side die. Usually, a significant number of people on the defeated side die. God is supposed to love all people, but our victory meant that He protected us and let the enemy get defeated. This is a clear manifestation of His will.

The same god who did not protect Jesus let Moses escape by granting him the power to part the Red Sea. But Moses didn't defeat the Egyptian army; he only fled from them. The Bible records that a strong wind blew, dividing the sea and allowing the Israelites to escape. But God supported me in winning the battle, and I was able to unify the country in less than ten years. In that sense, I feel that God loves me very much. And I think that my victory was surely a miracle. Furthermore, Islam steadily gained control of other countries and even had the power to convert entire Christian nations into Islamic nations. This was indeed an amazing miracle.

ISLAMIC RITUALS AND RELIGIOUS PRACTICES

The Koran itself is not a huge book, so Muslims refer to the Hadith—a record of my words and deeds, of how I acted, and what I judged to be good in different circumstances. This is the basic standard of conduct for Islam, since it would be a problem if people simply acted as they pleased. For example, Muslims face toward Mecca when they pray. If they stopped following this rule and started doing as they pleased—some turning toward Antarctica and others facing the North Pole—it would surely become a mess. The fact that Muslims all around the world turn toward Mecca to pray increases their sense of unity and their focus on God.

I believe that today, Islam is struggling because its strict precepts make it difficult to adapt to the changing times. When it comes to tradition, if you destroy one thing, everything collapses. In some cases, a whole race is destroyed when its people abandon faith in their god and their religion. This may have happened to Native Americans as well as the native tribes of Central and South America. I do think that some things should be changed, but we do risk losing things when we revise our traditions.

Ramadan and the Hajib

I think that non-Muslims often feel uncomfortable with our traditional practices. For example, Muslims fast during the month of Ramadan. But Buddhists fast, too. We actually took the idea of fasting from Buddhism—southwestern Asia is pretty close to India, after all. Ramadan is an example of how Islam has integrated Hindu and Buddhist spiritual practices. Fasting may be difficult if you are not used to it, but as a religious practice, I don't think it is strange at all.

Also, the scarves that the women wear (the hijab) have generated much controversy and have led to discrimination. It is a Muslim custom for women to cover their entire body, leaving only their eyes showing; women are not allowed to show their faces to men other than their husbands. From the Western perspective, this custom is disturbing. There is much concern over this issue, and in Europe, there is talk of banning the wearing of scarves. I admit that the Koran and the Hadith do teach that women should wear scarves, but I do not intend to force this practice on modern Muslims. In my day, we wore scarves in the desert because they protected us from the sun. We draped them from head to toe, primarily to prevent sunburn. I do not mind if people in other regions and climates wear other types of clothing.

We required women to wear the hijab because in those days, we basically lived in the kind of world depicted in *Ali Baba and the Forty Thieves*. Women were probably safe if they were not good-looking, but if they had a reasonably charming face and were attractive, they could have easily been taken by bandits. In short, women were in great danger of being kidnapped, so they covered their faces to make it difficult for men to evaluate their looks. Women were prohibited from showing their faces to men other than husbands so that other people wouldn't be able to tell what they looked like. The thieves would not want to kidnap a woman only to find out that she was a very old woman. So, one of the reasons we implemented that system was to protect women. The hijab is also a symbol of modesty, and as such, it is a cultural symbol of femininity. Westerners seem to have forgotten the concept of modesty; instead they seem to encourage women to "show" themselves. So the hijab is a cultural icon as well.

There are differences in perspectives and opinions, and every country goes through various kinds of change, and I believe we should accept this diversity to some extent. From the perspective of non-Muslims, it certainly might seem strange for a woman to cover her head with a black veil, but it is the same thing as how some Westerners think that Japanese students look odd when they wear school uniforms with stand-up collars, like soldiers or servants. I think that the Japanese schools give their students uniforms to minimize class distinctions; uniforms make it harder to judge what class a student is from. Uniforms also prevent students from getting distracted by fashion and choices about what to wear. So this is an issue of cultural difference.

Today, people wear suits and ties, but imagine if, for example, someone was wearing a necktie in fifteenth-century Japan: he would surely become a laughingstock. The people would certainly pick on him, saying, "What is the odd thing dangling around your neck?"

Dress is a custom, one aspect of human culture. When a certain culture begins to predominate over others, that culture's customs also gain influence, and when that culture dies out, so do its customs. So I don't think that everyone around the world should have to dress in exactly the same way.

I feel sad that Muslims in Europe are often discriminated against because of their ritual practices. People tend to think that Muslims are all suicide bombers. I wish to somehow facilitate more understanding.

Polygamy

I married my first wife, Khadija, when I was twenty-five. She was about forty years old, and when I founded my religion, she became my first supporter and patron. I was monogamous while she was alive. Even though polygamy was permitted, I stayed strictly monogamous out of fear. I persevered and endured the trial of monogamy for twenty-five years. After she died, God granted me permission to marry other women. I married many women who admired me as the founder of Islam, and I was blessed with many offspring. I believe this was a blessing from Allah. The children of my later marriages all went their separate ways and later formed the different sects of Islam, which resulted in the spread of Islam around the world.

I did not go to Hell, even though I married more than ten women. So I don't think monogamy is a teaching of God. It's more of a worldly issue, like contracts, rules, or precepts that have been formed out of jealousy. That's my understanding. It seems strange to me to determine whether a religion is good or evil based on its marriage system.

In this world, people have different opinions on polygamy. But as long as it doesn't involve any kind of criminal behavior, I don't see anything religiously improper about it. Jesus does not say anything in the Bible about monogamy. Monogamy is probably related to ancient Jewish beliefs. If you trace the ideology of monogamy, you will surely find that its roots are in Judaism. It was, in fact, a teaching for the working class in ancient Judea and did not apply to the nobility and the wealthy.

I believe that in the Old Testament, there is an account of a couple that could not bear children, so the husband was permitted to marry another wife. Since Abraham's wife, Sarah, was not able to have children, Sarah told her husband to take Hagar as a wife, so he married her. And God accepted this. But then, unexpectedly, when they were eighty or one hundred years old—I don't remember exactly how old they were, but certainly of advanced age—God told them that Abraham would have a child by Sarah, and this is indeed what came to pass. There are some rather unbelievable things recorded in the Old Testament, but these sorts of domestic challenges certainly existed.

In some cases, instead of marrying several women from their own social class, ancient Jewish men would take a female partner from the slave or servant class. This practice was probably not unique to the Jews, but was probably also an ancient Egyptian custom. In this kind of case, the husband could treat his new female partner differently from his wife. Moses's commandment prohibiting adultery did not apply to women from the so-called slave class, who were pledged to serve the men who owned them.

In short, I was not solely responsible for establishing the culture of polygamy. It already existed in the desert regions, including Egypt. Even the Buddha had four wives before he left them to become a monk. I believe Moses had more than two wives. I think even Jesus had two or three de facto wives. Socrates had two wives, too. And the maharajas in India and the wealthy men in Arabia also practiced polygamy.

As you can see, there are different styles of relationships. I think people should be able to talk among themselves and decide what to do, provided that the relationship is based on love for one another. I don't think the practice of polygamy should be the test that determines whether a religion is good or evil or whether it is guided by God or the Devil. When evaluating a religion, you need to carefully assess whether its teachings were fit for the time and place it was in and take into account the situations in which the teachings were given. I feel disappointed that our religion is judged to be evil just because of the marriage system we incorporated.

I had a good reason for endorsing polygamy for Muslims. During the period of relentless war between Medina and Mecca, many young men were killed, so many children were orphaned and many women were widowed. In the desert, if a woman was on her own or only with her children, without a man to protect her, she would die, most likely from hunger. So I encouraged women to remarry. I recommended that men who had the money to spare and were financially capable take in these widowed women. I wanted to make sure that they were taken care of, so I allowed my people to practice polygamy.

In short, the idea was that it was fine for those with sufficient resources or wealth to take on the care of others. Today, the government implements a progressive taxation system or other types of social welfare to take care of those who are less fortunate. In those days, however, such system did not exist, so you took care of others by taking them into your family.

In ancient times, it was common for a successful man to support all his relatives. In the same way, the system of polygamy was a type of social welfare, so I don't think it was entirely evil. Back then, it was basically impossible for women and children to live on their own. Of course there were some exceptions, such as my wife

Khadija, who owned and managed a trade caravan. There were talented women who were equivalent to today's female corporate CEO's. But in general, a large percentage of women had to receive support and protection to survive.

Of course, Christian nations would never accept such a system. But they also face some problems. More and more families are falling apart because they use monogamy as a criterion for determining good and evil. Also, the Christian concept of covenants has its good and bad sides. We cannot simply apply the same rule that binds God and humans to the relationship of two people. This may be fine in business and law, but when it comes to emotional matters, the rules differ from person to person. So I believe that it is better to adapt your perspective to what is best for the age you live in. Marriage is one of the experiences that we can go through in this world as part of our soul training, so I believe that we should be able to use our free will to choose a marriage system.

Women's Rights

On the other hand, I believe that Islam needs to reconsider and change its stance on women's rights. In Islam, one man can marry up to four women, but if a woman engages in any "free love" outside of official marriage, she may be sentenced to death. Christian nations criticize Muslims for the severity of this punishment. It is not in accord with modern understandings of human rights, so I think Muslims need to reconsider this issue.

Also, in Islam, there is still a culture of giving a daughter away in exchange for assets. Muslims still tend to see women as property, and parents do not usually allow their daughters to choose their husbands freely. The reason for this is that parents invest in their children until they reach adulthood. Children are a family investment. It is customary in the Arabic world for parents to receive a dowry proportionate to the cost of raising their daughter. So if, for example, a daughter falls in love with someone and marries him while she is studying abroad, the parents feel as though they've been robbed of the money that they invested in their daughter. Of course, this idea leads parents to treat their daughter as property, and some say that it is a violation of human rights. But this practice also encourages parents to raise their daughter with affection and care, since if they do, they will be sure to receive a dowry when she marries.

It is not so easy to lavish affection on your daughter if you know that she will eventually be "stolen away." It would be difficult for parents to keep providing for their daughter—spending money, sending her to school, paying tuition, buying beautiful clothes and make-up, and giving her everything she needs—only to have her taken away by some fellow she suddenly falls for. On the other hand, if you are offered twenty sheep as a dowry, for example, you may feel that it is a fair exchange. Or you may feel that your daughter is worth much more—perhaps one hundred sheep. In our culture, it is the duty of the father and brothers to carry out these kinds of negotiations.

There is an unwritten rule that if a woman is snatched away without an appropriate dowry, her brothers must find and kill the man. Having to place a bounty on someone and chase him all over the world sounds a little like something out of the Warring States period, but this "eye for an eye" mentality still remains. I am not entirely sure that this fits the modern context, though.

ON MILITARY SUCCESS AND WEALTH

The fact that my wife was one of the richest people in Mecca was a great blessing for the Islam's beginnings. Our activities would have been impossible without some sort of financial backing. Any religious activity requires financial support.

After all, I was like today's businessman working at a trading firm. In today's terms, I was like a good-looking businessman who was picked up by a rich patroness. I was able to start a religion because of the financial resources that my wife provided. Her finances also enabled me to establish credibility within the community and to hire servants.

We achieved military success largely due to the logistics team that I built. I had developed the skills necessary to do this during my fifteen years of leading merchants in camel caravans and engaging in trade. My work in commerce gave me excellent business sense. I conducted trade in Egypt, India, and as far away as China, so I knew how to make money and negotiate deals.

But in terms of spreading Islam, success did not come easily. It was extremely difficult to break through the polytheistic beliefs of the Quraysh tribe. We really struggled to get them to abandon their ancestral religion. In the end, it was because I was unexpectedly blessed with talent in military affairs that we were able to achieve victory. This seems to have had a lasting effect to this day: now, Muslims engage in terrorism and guerilla warfare around the world. If this is my fault, I am truly sorry about it. I feel bad when I see a housewife with dynamite strapped around her belly desperately lunging at her enemy. Muslim military tactics have not advanced much since my day. I wish they would use more modern methods.

I resemble Hermes in that I was successful in both battle and business. I had financial sense. As far as I can tell from the Bible, Jesus had little financial sense. He was a carpenter, but since we don't really hear of his financial success as a carpenter, he must not have been very dedicated to his job. He preached around the country free of charge, and he moved from one hideout to another while receiving only small amounts of financial support from various patrons. I think he was moving from place to place while the women around him prepared his food. By contrast, I assembled an army and waged wars, which shows that I was capable of building a logistics department and running an organization. To some people, the Islamic world today may seem impoverished, but our religion was actually infused with "merchant blood" from its beginnings.

I think wealth is important. In my time, people could build wealth through trade, but today, it depends largely on whether they can extract oil from their land. Eventually, the oil will be gone, and they will need to find a new resource. Otherwise, it will be difficult to survive in a desert region. They can't even raise animals unless there is an oasis nearby. I hope they can build more plants that convert salt water into drinking water. I would like to see them grow new kinds of crops or breed animals that could become a new source of protein. I would also like them to gain the technological capability to produce and manufacture new products and goods. I believe the era of living off oil is coming to a close. So I think we should start transforming the overall structure of our civilization now, before the oil runs out.

THE PRACTICE OF HUMILITY TOWARD GOD
As I have said, the teachings of Islam are based on the Christian Old and New Testaments. In the Book of Genesis, which is believed to have been written by Moses, the difference between God and humanity is very clear. God is depicted as the being who separated the heavens from the earth, created the world in six days, and rested on the seventh. Of course, I don't think that the world was actually created in six days; I believe that there is a symbolic element to this story. But this story shows that the gap between God

and humanity is extraordinarily large. Of course, there are also differences among human beings, from the king of a country and the
nobility to the ordinary citizens. But these variations are relatively
small in comparison with the huge gap between human beings and
God, who created the world and all creatures. God cannot possibly
be on the same level as human beings.

I wanted to strongly emphasize God's absolute power and supreme nature, so I stressed the importance of human humility before God. So even though people are all different—some are rich
while others are poor; some have high status while others have low
status—when standing before the one and only God, all people
must bow low, humbling themselves in prostration. People may
have different opinions on this issue, but I believe that we should
get down on bended knees before the one and only God, as a cour-
tesy, to show our respect to Him. And when people take a sub-
missive posture before God, they all become equal; this posture of
humility is a symbol of the equality of all people under God.

The modern Western idea of freedom is the freedom for human
beings to take the place of God. I believe people started thinking
this way as they gained more worldly knowledge. In the nineteenth
and twentieth centuries, human beings got too full of themselves
and even went so far as to say that God was a creation of human
beings—a figment of human imagination. I feel that people became conceited. Those who thought this way were intellectuals
and educators who guided others to believe it, as well. The spread
of this sort of ideology surely incurs the wrath of God and brings
consequences. So I believe that it is my job to inspire a feeling of
awe toward God and to awaken people to their original nature. For
that purpose, I think it is important for Islam to spread globally.

The biggest problem with what you call the free world is that it
lacks equality. It has become all about "the survival of the fittest."

If we emphasize equality under the one God, equality under the absolute God, or submission to the absolute God, we can reduce the disparities that this world of the survival of the fittest has created. And between these two principles, the view that distinguishes God from humans is better for developing people's faith. I don't think it is good for humans to get too close to God.

I feel a bit uncomfortable with the idea of "loving God." To me, it makes it sound as if God is your wife. I don't think we should treat God like that. God is the absolute being. It is more correct to say that human beings receive God's mercy than to say that human beings love God. The gap between God and humanity is tremendous. It is like the relationship between the sun and the earth. The sun may appear small to us, since we are far from it. But it is the heat and light of the sun, streaming down upon us incessantly and unilaterally, that allows all things to live. Plants and crops grow, and these in turn feed animals and human beings and allow them to live. In this way, we receive great blessings from the sun. The relationship between God and human beings is like the relationship between the sun and the earth. The earth may have some effect on the sun, but it is probably only to a small extent: the earth simply intercepts the sun's light somewhat by imbibing it. Perhaps the relationship between the sun and the planets is like that between a parent and children. Since the planets revolve around the sun, the sun may feel the type of love, affection, or intimacy that parents feel for their children.

In any case, I believe that there is an absolute gap between God and humanity. In my eyes, God is Allah, the All Merciful, who unilaterally pours down mercy upon human beings. Human beings can only worship Him, look up to Him, and dedicate ourselves to Him. In that sense, the Christian idea of "loving thy God," which is also an idea embraced in ancient Greece, seems to me like a seed of hubris that is about to sprout.

Moses repudiated the practice of idolatry, so the rejection of idol worship was not a new idea. But Muslims took this idea to somewhat of an extreme, and this might have caused trouble historically. For Muslims, worshipping a statue or an object as God is blasphemy. Muslims feel as though worshipping a statue of a human being as God lowers God to the level of human beings, so they reject this practice as idolatry. But I understand why people have different opinions about this.

VIOLENCE, REVOLUTION, AND THE SURVIVAL OF ISLAM

During roughly the same period that the West was going through modernization, we attempted various experiments to bring innovation to Islam, but without much lasting success. The height of our civilization had already passed. Islam flourished during the Middle Ages, but since the onset of the modern era, we have fallen behind. Instead, other religions have flourished. For example, Christianity, which had declined during the Middle Ages, regained its power. As a country, Japan and America both gained strength.

God's plan in all this is over my head. Civilizations rise and fall, and I cannot tell what will happen. But I believe that if Islam reaches an impasse as a religion, reforms will eventually take place. Islam now has more than one billion adherents and is still spreading. This means that many people find value in Islam. The fact that the number of Muslims is increasing shows that Islam is gaining popularity. While Christianity spread among those who pursued freedom, Islam is spreading among those who seek equality and submission to God. This probably means that these two principles are equally important for human beings.

When a religion establishes a particular style, that style might create problems, but on the other hand, it might also create results.

At the time of the founding of Islam, we engaged in conflict. If we had lost those conflicts, there would have been nothing left. A tiny, new religion would have appeared and been crushed, and that would have been the end of the story.

Religion is inherently revolutionary. How much power a religion exerts depends on whether its revolutionary potential remains ideological or is accompanied by military action. Islam is a religion, but in some sense, I think that it resembles communism. Communists have justified killing by saying that revolution is born from the barrel of a gun. In other words, communists prioritize the ends over the means. They are not saying that the end justifies the means. They are simply validating violent means. To say that revolution is born from the barrel of a gun is basically to say that you cannot bring about a revolution unless you kill people. A nation with this philosophy can instantly dominate other countries that are committed to peace or that take a conciliatory approach to conflict. That's what happened to Tibet.

Some say that Islam destroyed Buddhism in India, but that is because Buddhist monks abided by Shakyamuni's teaching of nonviolence, which prohibited them from fighting and killing. They behaved nobly as human beings, but their behavior allowed Islam to destroy Buddhism in the blink of an eye. Because of their commitment to nonviolence, Buddhists are easily defeated. Sometimes, to protect yourself, you have no choice but to kill your enemies. At those times, if you strictly follow the precept of nonviolence, you will be defeated. I believe the members of the Shakya clan were all massacred. Sometimes, you need to take just action to protect yourself. I understand that it is not always easy to tell which side justice is on, but it is also true that if you are defeated, you will vanish.

If you strictly adhere to nonviolence, you are basically doomed to destruction. The question is, is it okay with you if all of your fellow citizens are annihilated? If the answer is no, then you need to change your way of thinking. In the world of divinity, the many gods have a myriad of different opinions. But the majority of them would support the idea of protecting oneself against unjust aggression.

Even though Jesus became a sacrificial lamb, Christians attack their enemies fiercely. Jesus taught, "If anyone strikes you on the cheek, offer the other also" (Luke 6:29), but Christians will attack without hesitation. They are not really following Jesus's teachings. Their founder said, "If anyone takes away your coat, offer your shirt also" (Luke 6:29), and "If anyone forces you to go one mile, go also the second mile" (Matthew 5:41)—but Christians still attack their enemies. So I think it's okay to differentiate worldly matters from religious teachings. I believe we should allow a margin for interpretation of religious teachings so we can still do what needs to be done in this world, including the world of politics.

AUTHOR'S THOUGHTS

ALLAH AND EL CANTARE

Muhammad's calling began with the spiritual revelations he received in the mountains. But when the first spirit called upon him, Muhammad thought it was the evil jinn of the desert. It's only natural that he thought that; according to descriptions of his first revelation, his body shook and he broke into a cold sweat. These are the kinds of symptoms that I have experienced when evil spirits have come to me. Since he was a psychic, he could have experienced negative spiritual influences, too.

But considering the universality of Islam, which has spread to billions of people, it's probably safe to say that Muhammad was receiving the revelations from the prophets that were guiding the desert region. However, Muhammad could not tell who was sending the spiritual messages to him. Only a few prophets, if any, would have been able to identify which spirits were speaking to them. Even Jesus Christ didn't have a clear idea of who was actually sending him the messages he received. Moses and the other Jewish prophets couldn't identify the spirits that were speaking to them, either. That was why they called them all "God"—but they also referred to that god by different names, such as Yahweh, Jehovah, and Elohim. Similarly, Muhammad couldn't tell who was speaking to him, so he said that it was Allah.

It requires an exceptionally high level of spiritual awareness to identify spirits, comprehend their characters, and understand their opinions on different matters. In fact, one of the distinctive characteristics of the spiritual communication that I now engage in is that

I can clearly identify the spirits who are in contact with me. This is quite rare in the history of humankind. As far as I know, I am the only one who can do this.

So, like other prophets, Muhammad couldn't really tell who was sending him the messages he was receiving, and at first, he thought they were from Allah, the god of the Middle East. But then Christians told him that God is too great to directly communicate with human beings and that He only sends revelations through angels. So Muhammad started saying that he had received the revelations through Jibril, the archangel Gabriel, who was responsible for delivering heavenly messages to Earth. But in fact, he wasn't actually able to discern who it was that was sending him the messages. The truth was that a group of divine spirits were sending the messages to Muhammad. I was actually one of them.

The god of creation had been worshipped on the Arabian Peninsula since pre-Islamic times. Allah is not a name of God; it is a general term meaning "god of creation." This is evident from the fact that Muhammad's father's name was Abd Allah, which means "servant of God." In the Middle Eastern faith, the name of the god of creation was Elohim. Elohim was the god that people in the Middle East commonly believed in before Islam appeared. Elohim is the god whom we now refer to as El Cantare. El Cantare sent Muhammad to Earth with the same mission as that of the Jewish and Christian prophets: to convey His teachings to people. The fact that He guided Judaism, Christianity, and Islam illustrates the magnanimity of El Cantare.

During a spiritual conversation I had with Muhammad, I asked him who he thought Allah was—if he thought Allah was Yahweh or Jehovah, and whether Allah was also the god of Judaism or the god of Christianity. He said that he believes that Allah is actually El Cantare. He said that the god he believes in is El Cantare, but that it is not easy for him to pull back from a fight that has continued for more than two thousand years. So it seems that to solve this conflict and bring about a resolution, we must increase awareness of and faith in the higher god, El Cantare.

MUHAMMAD'S CONTRIBUTIONS AND LIMITATIONS

Muhammad's accomplishment was to bring innovation to the world of religion. At that time, people in the Middle East worshipped gods of stones and trees among many other gods. If they had stayed as they were, it would have been difficult for them to develop a more advanced religion. Muhammad's revolutionary movement cleaned up primitive beliefs and built faith in a superior god. Muhammad was then able to unify people under a shared faith in the same god. Overall, it was a revolutionary movement that promoted systematical disposal of primitive beliefs and brought advancement to the religious world. However, this movement caused a lot of bloodshed. The Quraysh didn't accept Muhamad's denial of their faith and so attacked Muhammad fiercely. Muhammad definitely contributed to the advancement to religion, but his understanding of God was not complete.

Many divine spirits or High Spirits reside in Heaven, and many of them are revered as gods around the world. So it is not right to believe that there is only one god and that all the other gods are fake. However, it is also true that different gods are on different levels and that El Cantare is the Supreme God guiding the planet Earth. Although there is a hierarchy of gods, I believe that it is best that all religions develop and prosper while maintaining harmony with one another.

EQUALITY AND FREEDOM

During a spiritual conversation, I asked Muhammad what one idea he would most like to spread. His answer was equality. He said he would like to spread the idea of equality among human beings. A monotheistic faith, he said, teaches that only God should be revered—that all human beings are equal under God, so no one should be arrogant.

I believe that people should have equal opportunities to succeed. To that end, we sometimes need to make adjustments so that the gap between people does not become too wide. Human beings have an inherent wish for equality, so the concept of equality may serve the good of the people. However, if you have to choose between freedom and equality, choosing freedom will lead you to greater happiness. This example may be a little extreme, but if it is purely equality that leads to happiness, you could say that prison inmates must be happy because they are equal. They are treated equally in prison: they eat the same breakfast, lunch and dinner; wear the same clothes; sleep in the same place; and work the same hours. But if you were one of those inmates, would you say that you are happy because you are equal to the other inmates? Certainly, you would not. You would be unhappy because you are being deprived of freedom. People suffer more from losing their freedom than from losing their equality. You can imagine how happy prison inmates feel when they are released from prison. Deprivation of freedom is a severe punishment.

With freedom, you have a chance to become the president of a country or end up a beggar. This kind of freedom may create an unequal society, in a sense. But from another perspective, freedom provides us with a chance to test ourselves in this world. You have the freedom to start a company, save up money, run for Congress, and aim for the presidency, but there is always the possibility that you will start a company only to go bankrupt and become homeless. You may face a severe consequence as a result of the choices you make—but it is still better to have freedom than equality.

Of course, safety-net programs should be provided to help those who aren't able to survive in a competitive world. We need to create a society in which the government and the affluent have a spirit of charity and help the underprivileged maintain a minimum standard of wholesome and cultured living. However, we do not have to create a society in which everyone gets equal results.

Today, the majority of Islamic nations are impoverished, with the exception of a few affluent oil-producing countries. If Islam is going to spread the concept of equality, I believe that it will replace communism in establishing an equality of poverty.

THE FUTURE OF THE ISLAMIC NATIONS
I have no intention of denying Islam. But Muslims' belief that everything happens according to the will of Allah is making them lose the spirit of self-help. I believe that self-help efforts will improve the Islamic nations. Instead of solely attributing their poverty to God's will, Muslims can improve their situation by studying more, working harder, and trying to come up with creative solutions to the problems that face them.

I believe that my native country, Japan, should help Islamic countries prosper by providing them with technological assistance. Japanese companies can invest in Islamic nations, and the Japanese government can implement policies to support these nations. We would also like to spread our new spiritual movement, Happy Science, which draws on the Japanese tradition of integrating diverse values while maintaining a strong faith, so that we can prevent Islamic nations and Christian nations from engaging in a full-blown final battle. We would like to spread new teachings that will mediate between and reconcile Islam and Christianity so that together, we can create a new era of spirituality.

Eternal Truths for a Happy World

I. Eternal Truths for a Changing Society

As I look back on the journey that brought me to where I am today, I see that I have come a long way since the early years of developing my spiritual philosophy. I delivered my first lecture when I was thirty years old. Since then, I have given more than 2,300 lectures, published more than 1,700 books, and produced several films. In recent years, the momentum of my ministry has stepped up considerably due to my tours to our temples in Japan and abroad. I have kept up an intense pace of giving lectures at least once a week. Many people are astonished that I'm able to keep going at such a speed and constantly keep my passion aflame. Sometimes it is a wonder to me, too. When I think about it, I believe that everything I've done has been made possible by the sense of mission and duty that continues to burn from deep within me. People often ask how I am able to keep my sense of duty alive so continually. The only way I can describe it is by saying that there is a part of me that believes that I myself *am* a mission. I am my mission; my mission is what my life is made of.

Civilization has achieved great scientific and technological advancement. But despite our progress, we have lost perhaps the most important type of knowledge that matters for our happiness: spiritual knowledge. Humans are essentially spiritual beings, and as spiritual beings, they inhabit physical bodies to live on Earth. This is a basic truth that everyone must know. This truth has been taught by the major world religions and in fundamental philosophies of the past. This same concept is conveyed not only by large religions but also by the smaller, ethnic religions in each country. This is a very simple truth that all religions teach.

But even those who respect religions and faiths and believe in the spirit world and spirits need to learn the Truths, because they probably have not studied it properly. Times have changed since the world religions were founded two thousand or more years ago. Everywhere we look, we are surrounded by advancements that would have been unimaginable back then. But despite repeated religious reform, many religions do not offer answers to the questions that modern life raises. And some religious teachings have simply become so arcane that they do not even apply to today's world. We are living in a new age, and that new age requires new ways of thinking that will serve as the foundation for the new society we wish to build.

The universal Truths that are common to many religions have the power to lead people to happiness, but only if we truly understand them. It is our misunderstandings of religious teachings, not the spiritual Truths themselves, that have led to the terrorism and war that have caused so many people to distance themselves from religion. There would be no conflict at all if we all had a better understanding of the world's religions and God's Truths.

For example, Shakyamuni Buddha's teachings have been passed down through scriptures called sutras for 2,500 years. But only part of them have survived and today's Buddhists only practice some of the Truths. Meanwhile, many Buddhist teachings have degenerated into mere formalities devoid of spiritual awareness. In ceremonies, Buddhists still recite sutras but they were written and translated so long ago that it is impossible for modern people to understand them. Moreover, many of the Buddhist monks who perform funeral ceremonies do not even believe in the soul or the afterlife.

Christianity is facing a similar problem. Many Christians do not believe that miracles can happen today, because in their minds, the teachings of Jesus Christ were frozen in time two thousand years ago. For example, Joan of Arc protected France from British invasion, but it took the Catholic Church hundreds of years to recognize the many miracles she performed and to canonize her. Christians may believe that the Father in Heaven and other prophets spoke to Jesus, and they may believe that Jesus and his disciples performed miracles, but they are hesitant to believe in anything that has happened since biblical times. Because people have stopped believing in miracles, they have stopped occurring in Christian churches, and because Christian ministers no longer believe in miracles, they talk about little other than how the Bible should be interpreted.

Christians have also faced many challenges regarding the modernization of their teachings. In some cases, Christian teachings have been at odds with scientific research and medicine. It took the Catholic Church hundreds of years to accept the theories of Galileo and Copernicus. When we address cases like the heliocentric theory of the structure of the solar system, the Bible should not be our source for Truth, and we should instead look at scientific experiments and observations to determine what is correct. Once scientific progress is made, the truth becomes undeniably clear. In this case, once we flew into outer space, there was no denying that the heliocentric theory was correct.

Over the centuries, scientists discovered many facts that contradicted biblical teachings. As a result, many people turned away from Christianity and toward atheism and materialism. Even many Christians have begun to follow practical science even while they continue to call themselves Christians. Many of them are probably Christian only in name because they want to secure their graves and funerals.

Shakaymuni Buddha and Jesus both taught that the soul is our true nature and that we are living in this physical world only temporarily. These Truths will never change. But the way we live in this world and the various workings of society have gone through tremendous transformations. Those of us who are living now should be asking ourselves, in the spirit of true Buddhists and true Christians, what Shakyamuni Buddha would say if he were alive today, and what Jesus Christ would say if he were alive today.

The founders of our established religions did not address many of the problems we face today for the simple reason that these problems did not exist thousands of years ago. To deal with modern problems, we need new teachings that are based on universal ways of thinking and that encourage objective self-reflection as a path to happiness. We need new perspectives and opinions to help us judge between right and wrong and to provide answers and solutions to our problems in a timely manner.

It is this belief that has been the source of the sense of duty I feel to use today's language to explain and spread the Truths to today's people. This is where my drive comes from, and this is what keeps me going every single day.

II. The Roots of Religious Conflict

HEAVEN'S PLAN FOR GLOBAL HAPPINESS: EVOLVING RELIGIONS WITH ETERNAL TRUTHS

If God exists, why is there fighting between people of different religions? If there is only one God, why are we killing each other? In my quest for answers to these questions, I learned that God has sent a group of heavenly spirits at the start of every new age to give fresh teachings that will guide people to happiness. These spirits have created many religions because they wish for us to have the kind of happiness that we can gain during our physical lives and then take with us to the afterlife. In a civilization experiment, many religious leaders were sent to Earth to create teachings for designated regions and ages. The differences in their personalities led to the variation among the different religions. Since God has created many religions to teach happiness, we can see common Truths shared across many religions throughout the world and throughout history. We should not focus on the differences between ideologies. Instead, we should discover and appreciate the Truths that are essential to all of our lives and that apply universally to everyone's happiness. It is essential that we develop a macro perspective on the world, for a broader worldview is the key to discovering God's profound plan for humanity and finally bringing our world together in unity.

COMPETITION, MONOTHEISM, AND MISUNDERSTANDING

After different religious leaders have expounded and spread their religions, heavenly spirits have watched over Earth to find out how much happiness the different teachings have created. Many divine spirits in Heaven are earnestly watching the progress the world has made as a result of the work of religious leaders and the religions that developed from them. The different spirits continue to guide the religions that they are in charge of, working night and day to find teachings that suit the people of our times.

There is a naturally competitive spirit among the different divine spirits. But neither spirits nor human believers should ever take competitiveness to an extreme. The goal of competition is never to create hatred or war or to completely dominate other religions. A certain degree of friendly competition, stimulation, and constructive criticism is valuable for preventing corruption and degeneration. But it should always be based on religious tolerance and should never develop into persecution, anger, envy, disdain, or ideas that are contrary to the will of God.

One of the causes of religious conflict has been the belief that only one religion can be right. This belief is mistaken, but it arose for a reason. To avoid confusion when religions were created, sometimes one god was designated the main god for a particular religion. This practice led to, for example, Islam's monotheistic belief that Allah is the one and only God, which has motivated the actions of Islamic fundamentalists as they have tried to destroy other faiths. Islamic extremists have used rocket artillery to destroy the great Buddhas of Bamiyan because they believe that idol worship is wrong. Christianity's monotheism probably led former American president George W. Bush to believe that Islam is an evil religion. It is possible that he felt little sympathy for the Muslims when he decided to wage assaults on Arab countries. This kind of violence has occurred because of wrong interpretations of the teachings and despite the fact that Christianity and Islam were originally sister religions.

THE DIVINE SPIRITS OF HEAVEN

My belief in God and divine beings has some similarity to monotheism, but it has similarities to polytheistic religions, too. I have found from actual experience that there is a spirit whom I call the Highest God, who is the most holy and venerated being. This may be similar to the monotheistic idea of a Creator God. And I have discovered that below this Highest God are many divine spirits who possess holiness beyond ordinary human levels and deserve to be called gods. The population of the world is so enormous that we need many gods to share the responsibility of making the world happy.

I have been visited by many gods of ethnic and polytheistic religions; these gods are sometimes known as angels, bodhisattvas, or *tathagatas*. None of these gods is fake; all are divine spirits in their own right. Each of these gods has a unique personality, and each once lived on Earth and worked to help people spiritually. Their accomplishments on Earth were so holy and were respected by so many people that when they returned to the afterlife, they became divine beings who were venerated as gods or buddhas. I often refer to these gods as divine spirits, angels, archangels, bodhisattvas, or *tathagatas*. In Heaven, these divine spirits reside on various levels and decrease in number as we ascend through the levels.

So the truth is that many of the ethnic and polytheistic gods around the world are neither fake nor evil. People of different faiths believe in a god or in many gods, as befits their religion's size and characteristics. My belief in the existence of many divine beings accords with the many polytheistic religions that have existed throughout the world, including in ancient Egypt, Greece, Rome, and India. When Judaism, Christianity, and Islam developed the idea that only their God was the right one and deemed other gods fake or evil, it may have led their missionary work to spread widely, but it also led to hatred that in turn led to wars. Many interreligious wars have been caused by this ignorance about the existence of many divine beings.

Heaven has many gods who take on different responsibilities and roles, and among them are leaders or teachers who guide and supervise large groups of other gods. So when a religion is created, a guiding spirit is placed in charge of assisting the religious founder on Earth. Which god is placed in charge depends on the era, region, and nature of the new religion. There have been times when a guiding spirit has instructed the founder to follow only that spirit's own guidance, but they were not implying that all other gods were false.

JUDAISM, CHRISTIANITY, AND ISLAM

Judaism is a monotheistic religion whose god is Yahweh, a god that is prone to jealousy and tends to forbid his people from be-

lieving in any other god. Yet if we look closely, we see that Yahweh is not the only god who appears in the Hebrew Bible; another
spirit, Elohim, makes many appearances, too. Yahweh is the spirit
I call Enlil, and Elohim is the spirit I call El Cantare; I have written about both of these spirits in previous books. Both of them
were guiding Judaism, which means that Judaism is actually led
by more than one god.

Unfortunately, when Yahweh was guiding Judaism especially
earnestly, he may have forbidden his people from believing in any
other deity, perhaps to help those who believed in religions that
were harmful to them. But this did not mean that no other gods
existed besides him. Of course, it is important to teach people not
to worship evil or harmful gods. But to interpret this as meaning
that all other religions and gods are wrong would naturally result in
a great deal of confusion.

Judaism's faith in Yahweh developed when many of the early
Jewish prophets, including Moses, gave teachings about him. But
in the Hebrew Bible, the name of God changes to Elohim when
two prophets appear, both with the name Isaiah. In fact, faith in
Elohim preceded Judaism. It was a large, established faith throughout the Middle East and Africa, while Judaism was a small religion
practiced only by the Jews. Elohim began to guide the new Jewish
prophets because plans were set up to establish a larger and more
global faith than Judaism through Christianity, eight hundred years
into the future. These new prophets were sent to pave the way for
Christianity to take root, under Elohim's guidance. The Jews did
not realize that Elohim was not Yahweh, though, and assumed that
both names referred to the same being.

Since most of us cannot see the spirit world with our physical
eyes, we can only try to understand God through teachings that
have been passed down in writing or orally. Religious leaders face a

similar challenge. Many of the conflicts we face today are a product of the difficulty that religious leaders faced in identifying which and how many spirits were talking to them.

We need certain spiritual abilities to correctly identify which spirit is speaking to us. Most religious leaders were able to hear divine spirits but not see them. For example, some religions forbid the worship of statues or physical representations of the divine. This teaching was created by religious leaders who were unable to see the spirits who were guiding them and could only hear the divine voices or write them down through automatic writing. I assure you that had they had the ability to see the divine beings that came to speak to them, they would have been inspired to try to express those beings' images in some physical form, such as statues or paintings. They would have wanted to share with others what the divine spirits looked like.

Jesus Christ studied the Hebrew Bible, and he, like the Hebrew prophets, was unable to make a clear distinction between Yahweh and Elohim. But the God he believed in was Elohim, the God of love, who was still being worshiped throughout the Middle East during Jesus's lifetime. The conservative Jews who adhered to traditional Judaism ended up persecuting Jesus.

Islam is also monotheistic. Muslims believe in Allah. But the Koran is a compilation of the teachings that Muhammad received through spiritual messages, and when we take a close look at it, we see that some passages use the plural "we" to refer to the spirit who is talking, while other passages use the singular "I." Muslims interpret this discrepancy simply as variations in the way Allah refers to himself. But the truth is that "we" refers to an entire group of guiding spirits whose members were taking turns sending messages to Muhammad. As with Judaism, even though Muslims believe that their religion is monotheistic, in truth, Islam was guided by many spirits. One main spirit may have been in charge, but a group of spirits took turns guiding Muhammad.

In later centuries, conflicts between Christianity and Islam developed. But the ironic truth is that Elohim was guiding Islam during its development, too. Christians and Muslims believed in the same God, but misunderstandings between the two religions have kept them in conflict. Combined with Islam's denial of the worship of statues, and each side's claim that their God is the only God, these misunderstandings caused Elohim's true teachings to become confused. The two religions became disordered, and the confusion led to multiple wars.

RELIGION AND VIOLENCE

In fact, many world religions have been war-oriented. Christianity has a history of following a military philosophy, which in many countries has developed into a readiness for war. This is contradictory to Jesus's teachings in the Bible: "If anyone strikes you on the right cheek, turn the other also" (Matthew 5:39). I believe that this contradiction was caused by Christians' study of the Hebrew Bible together with the New Testament.

The philosophy of the separation of church and state is probably another reason that Christian nations have been prone to war. When someone asked Jesus whether or not to pay taxes to Caesar, he pointed to the image of Caesar on a coin and asked, "Whose likeness and inscription is this?" When the questioner responded, Jesus said: "Give therefore to the emperor the things that are the emperor's, and to God the things that are God's" (Matthew 22:20-21). This developed into the concept of the separation of church and state, which became a way for Christian nations to justify military action, even though it contradicted Jesus's other teachings.

This is another example of the way interpretations of religious teachings have conflicted with the secular interests of governments and economies.

The Islamic world has also been prone to fighting. In recent years, Islamist terrorist attacks have been rattling the world, and this alarming violence has brought to light the need for reforms to Islam. The frequency and number of attacks have been so high that it is difficult to believe that the problem lies only with the extremists. The Muslims involved in the fighting believe that they are following the words of God, and this problem needs to be addressed. Islam's justification for war lies in Muhammad's history of waging war and achieving military victory. As a result, the justification of war as a means to an end has become a major part of the Islamic world. This philosophy is similar to Mao Zedong's communism. Because China is officially based on materialism and atheism, it constantly violates human rights—human beings there are seen as only material, like robots, and therefore as expendable. We need to look into this further and also find ways to reform Islamic nations to help them coexist with the Christian world and the rest of the world.

III. Uniting the World Under a Spiritual Perspective

To create positive change and a brighter future, the world's religions must be able to provide right opinions in a timely manner on important issues of the day. It is our duty to encourage religious and social reform and innovation based on ideal religious principles.

I aim to prevent the struggle between Islam and Christianity from becoming a full-blown war and to lead the different religions to harmonious coexistence as we all make progress together. I am working to establish teachings that will both integrate diverse values and establish strong faith. El Cantare is the most venerated God, the head of other gods, and possesses supreme spiritual awareness. But he is not the only God. Beneath him, countless divine beings variously known as gods, archangels, angels, *tathagatas*, and bodhisattvas are working as a team, with divided roles and responsibilities, to carry out a common goal.

The world needs to practice compassionate religious tolerance toward diverse religions. We must come together in a belief in the God of love and compassion, El Cantare. El Cantare is working earnestly to guide the world to the right path. His teachings of self-reflection and repentance will help everyone find the right path again.

The world also needs spiritual knowledge about where our souls came from and where we will go in the afterlife. It is essential for our happiness to know that we are spiritual beings living temporarily inside physical bodies as part of our soul training. No matter how much knowledge we gain, we will not gain true wisdom and we will never be able to find our way home until we know where we came from and where we are headed. It is the same as needing to know our parents' phone numbers or our home address to find our way back. Many of us today do not know these basic facts or else misunderstand them. But if we can learn them with an open mind, we will be able to live rightly, from that higher spiritual awareness that we call enlightenment.

IV. The Fourfold Path to Happiness

It is essential for everyone to know that the soul is who we really are. Our physical bodies are temporal existences that will perish when we pass on to the afterlife, but our souls will continue to exist in the other world. When we pass on to the other world, we will determine which part of the other world we belong to, Heaven or Hell, by watching our own lives as they are played in front of us like a film on a movie screen. There are many walks of life and infinitely different ways of living. So there is no one who has lived a perfect life and no one who lived a completely wrong life. What matters is how we judge ourselves in the final analysis, whether we decide that our lives were filled with more good or more bad.

Every day of our lives is part of our journey toward the other world. We must ask ourselves: Has my life so far been in tune with Heaven, so that I would not seem out of place if I were to visit Heaven's angels right now? Or would I blend in with the darker world of Hell if I were to visit it today? It is important, as we go about our daily lives, to be aware of the afterworld and to always be mindful of our state of mind, because these are the things that determine who we are and where we will go in the afterlife.

I recommend practicing four principles: love, wisdom, self-reflection, and progress. These four principles are guidelines for living. Practicing them every day ensures a happy and meaningful life. Together, I call these principles "The Principles of Happiness" or sometimes "The Modern Fourfold Path."

Each of the Principles of Happiness depends on a foundation of faith. Faith is essential to our happiness. We must cherish our capacity for faith, because it is a completely unique ability that was given to us as part of the human condition. There must be a reason why animals cannot practice faith but we humans can.

LOVE

One of the paths to happiness lies in being a giver of love, not a taker. We all want to be loved; it is part of human nature. But the people of Heaven rarely think about getting love; instead, they are always thinking about giving love. The purpose of practicing the principle of love is to become a giver who loves unconditionally everyone who is with us in this age, regardless of the gains or losses our love might involve us in.

We can love others by discovering their wonderful traits. We can also love others by realizing that everyone has the right to happiness and so helping people live splendid lives. We can also give love by finding joy in other people's happiness and success—for example, feeling joy when we see people smile, become wealthy, find their way onto the right path, and find happiness. So let's try to be givers, not takers, of love on our path to happiness.

WISDOM

The Principle of Wisdom is the second Principle of Happiness. The aim of practicing this principle is to develop the kind of wisdom that enables you to explain the relationship between this world and the other world. This is not the only kind of wisdom that matters for life in the modern world, but it is by far the most important. It is also valuable, for example, to learn and understand diverse worldviews. But it is absolutely essential to have proper spiritual knowledge that you can take with you to the other world.

We all have to work, many of us must support a family, and we also have many other responsibilities. So sometimes, we get caught up in the hustle and bustle of everyday life and lose our spiritual perspective. As we live each day, we should think about God's perspective and ask ourselves whether we are living the right way—that is, whether we are being mindful of our spiritual nature. It is valuable to remind ourselves as often as possible that we are spiritual beings living in this physical world and that there is another world that we will eventually journey on to.

The aim of practicing the Principle of Wisdom is to empower ourselves with the wisdom and knowledge we need to live rightly—that is, to live in a way that creates happiness for ourselves and others. For example, a spiritual perspective helps my followers discover the many hints to life that are scattered throughout my lectures and spiritual messages. Living with a spiritual perspective enables us all to turn our knowledge and experiences into wisdom that helps us live splendid lives.

SELF-REFLECTION

The Principle of Self-Reflection is the third Principle of Happiness. Catholics are taught to repent through confession, and Catholic churches have confessional rooms where Catholics confess their sins and ask for forgiveness. Repentance through self-reflection is different. Self-reflection is a process in which we face ourselves alone, every day, without self-deprecation or self-condemnation. The aim is always happiness. We reflect upon our actions, our words, our thoughts, and our habitual patterns of thought. We consider all these things in light of God's Truths and try to determine within ourselves whether they have been right or wrong.

Even though we cannot see it physically, our minds contain a record of every thought, action, and experience we have ever had. This record is what will be played on the movie screen when we return to the other world. Your family, friends, mentors, and teachers who are living in the other world and the spirits who have been guiding you will all be watching this film with you. The film is condensed into an hour or two, and when it is over, we judge for ourselves whether our lives were filled with good.

This is when we find out whether we lived our life successfully or whether mistakes weighed us down. The reactions of our family and friends will also help us make a decision about whether we belong to Heaven or whether we should spend some time in training in Hell. Our decision will be based on which world is most appropriate for the way we lived our life.

There are many paths through Heaven and many paths through Hell; it is just a matter of choosing which path is best for our soul training. For example, those who committed murders and violent acts for no just cause and purely out of destructive emotion will most likely choose the path of self-reflection and decide to live in a world inhabited by similar people. The world we return to in our afterlife will be a place full of people with the same dominant tendencies as ours. As the murderers live surrounded by many people who are mirror images of themselves, the time will come when they will see their flaws reflected back to them.

Therefore, self-reflection is a principle of salvation. It gives us a chance to reflect on our mistakes in light of the Truths and repent for our errors while we are still in this world. We do not have to wait until an afterlife in Hell; we have the power to save ourselves, and we can begin right now.

The angels, bodhisattvas, and *tathagatas* in Heaven are always waiting to extend their helping hands and provide the light of Heaven to people who are making the effort to change and save themselves. Many religions oversimplify the teachings to try to make it easier to be saved. But I believe that to achieve true salvation, we need to have a full understanding of the mistakes we have made. We attain salvation by becoming aware of who we really are. Believing in Christ, for example, will not erase our sins unless we can take our repentance further and realize on our own what mistakes we have made. As our self-reflection progresses, the record in our minds will gradually change; our sins will be erased. When we watch our lives being played on the movie screen, the audience will applaud us every time we progress in our self-salvation by using self-reflection to discover and conquer our flaws.

PROGRESS

The last principle is the Principle of Progress. Practicing progress means aiming to spread happiness to the rest of society, the rest of our country, and the whole world as we strive to build a utopian Heaven on Earth. We must not keep to ourselves the happiness we achieve through our enlightenment; we must use our happiness to benefit the world around us. The happiness we achieve gives us the power to be constructive and to chase our dreams.

THE FOURFOLD PATH

Living by these four principles of love, wisdom, self-reflection, and progress—the Fourfold Path—will guarantee our return to Heaven in the afterlife, because this way of life empowers us to find our own way to Heaven. It is a path of self-salvation; there is no need for someone else to save us. The gates of Heaven will welcome us back if we live each day practicing the Fourfold Path and staying mindful of God's eyes.

We all have within ourselves the power to change, to create ourselves anew, and to build a future that represents our dreams and ideals. This power comes from the fragment of God inside us, which I call "divine nature." We are all children of God. Even if you are struggling with a darkness that looms within your mind right now, the child of God within you has the power to save you— all you have to do is awaken it. This knowledge is so essential for everyone's happiness that I feel it to be my duty, as someone who has discovered its tremendous power, to share it and help people awaken.

People who have grasped this Truth have experienced miracles of healing; once they realized the Truth, demons could no longer take hold of their minds. These miracles did not happen through my power. People created these miracles on their own by filling their minds with light and expelling the darkness within them. That is why I believe strongly that we all have the power to save ourselves.

V. Building a Happy Future for the World

Our history of religious conflict has taught us an important lesson: to accept diverse peoples and different ways of thinking. It is always difficult for older establishments to accept new ones. But we should not let our emotions carry us away. Instead, we should be rational, try to discern right from wrong, and resolve to accept teachings that are right as right and reject teachings that are wrong as wrong.

It may be an enormous and lofty challenge to try to coexist harmoniously with Christianity, Islam, and other religions around the world, but I believe that we have already conquered the first step to this challenge, because our philosophy and our way of thinking is already universal; it transcends religious boundaries. Believing in these Truths inherently commits us to establishing them globally. No matter how many decades, centuries, or millennia it takes, there will always be people who will teach that the world is one, that humankind is one. There will always be people who will spread the word that the teachings of God will save the world, including the whole of humankind. Eventually, these teachings will reach far to the ends of the world. They will be passed down to our children and to our children's children, and they will keep spreading without rest and without end.

My dream is to leave behind teachings that will cross religious boundaries, teachings powerful enough to create a world where everyone lives with love, acceptance, peace, and freedom. The inability to understand one another has resulted in the hatred, anger, and distrust that have caused religious conflicts. I hope that this movement I have created will solve these problems at their source and finally bring religious conflict to an end.

Reincarnation is one of the Truths that I have discovered about our souls. Reincarnation means that we may have been born in many different countries in our past lives. Someone who was born in Europe in this life may have been born in the United States, China, Korea, and Japan in past lives. Therefore, it's meaningless to feel hatred against any group of people, just as it's meaningless to believe that Heaven will guide only a select group of people or a single race or country—for we could have been one of "them" in a past life. In addition, it is not God's nature to be selective or exclusive. God never labels one group good and everyone else evil. God is powerful enough to guide everyone.

As the world's population keeps increasing, it becomes all the more important that we create a world in which people do not have to fear the future. My dream is for more and more people around the world, in every country, to be able to say that they are happy.

ABOUT THE AUTHOR

MASTER RYUHO OKAWA started receiving spiritual messages from Heaven in 1981. Holy beings appeared before him with impassioned messages of urgency, entreating him to deliver God's words to Earth. Within the same year, Master Okawa's deepest subconscious awakened and revealed his calling to become a spiritual leader who inspires the world with the power of God's Truths. Through these conversations with divine beings and through profound spiritual contemplation, Master Okawa developed the philosophy that would become the core of his teachings. His communications with Heaven deepened his understanding of God's designs and intentions—how He created our souls, this world, the other world, and the Laws that are the very fabric of the universe. In 1986, Master Okawa founded Happy Science to share God's Truths and to help humankind overcome religious and cultural conflicts and usher in an era of peace on Earth. The universality and integrity of his spiritual teachings, delivered in his uniquely simple and pragmatic way, have attracted millions of readers and followers in over one hundred countries. In addition to publishing over 1,700 books, Master Okawa has delivered more than 2,300 talks and lectures (as of October 18, 2014), and continues to share God's Truths throughout the world.

ABOUT HAPPY SCIENCE

In 1986, Master Ryuho Okawa founded Happy Science, a spiritual movement dedicated to bringing greater happiness to humankind by overcoming barriers of race, religion, and culture and by working toward the ideal of a world united in peace and harmony. Supported by followers who live in accordance with Master Okawa's words of enlightened wisdom, Happy Science has grown rapidly since its beginnings in Japan and now extends throughout the world. Today, it has twelve million members around the globe, with faith centers in New York, Los Angeles, San Francisco, Tokyo, London, Sydney, Sao Paulo, and Hong Kong, among many other major cities. Master Okawa speaks at Happy Science centers and travels around the world giving public lectures. Happy Science provides a variety of programs and services to support local communities. These programs include preschools, after-school educational programs for youths, and services for senior citizens and the disabled. Members also participate in social and charitable activities, which in the past have included providing relief aid to earthquake victims in China, New Zealand, and Turkey, and to flood victims in Thailand as well as building schools in Sri Lanka.

PROGRAMS AND EVENTS

Happy Science faith centers offer regular events, programs, and seminars. Join our meditation sessions, video lectures, study groups, seminars, and book events. Our programs will help you:

- Deepen your understanding of the purpose and meaning of life

- Improve your relationships as you learn how to love unconditionally
- Learn how to calm your mind even on stressful days through the practice of contemplation and meditation
- Learn how to overcome life's challenges. . . and much more.

INTERNATIONAL SEMINARS

Each year, friends from all over the world join our international seminars, held at our faith centers in Japan. Different programs are offered each year and cover a wide variety of topics, including improving relationships, practicing the Eightfold Path to enlightenment, and loving yourself, to name just a few.

HAPPY SCIENCE MONTHLY

Read Master Okawa's latest lectures in our monthly booklet, Happy Science Monthly. You'll also find stories of members' life-changing experiences, news from Happy Science members around the world, in-depth information about Happy Science movies, book reviews, and much more. Happy Science Monthly is available in English, Portuguese, Chinese, and other languages. Back issues are available upon request. Subscribe by contacting the Happy Science location nearest you.

CONTACT INFORMATION

Happy Science is a worldwide organization with faith centers around the globe. For a comprehensive list of centers, visit the worldwide directory at www.happy-science.org or www.happyscience-na.org.

The following are some of the many Happy Science locations:

UNITED STATES AND CANADA

New York

79 Franklin Street
New York, NY 10013
Phone: 212-343-7972
Fax: 212-343-7973
Email: ny@happy-science.org
website: newyork.happyscience-na.org

Los Angeles

1590 E. Del Mar Blvd.
Pasadena, CA 91106
Phone: 626-395-7775
Fax: 626-395-7776
Email: la@happy-science.org
website: losangeles.happyscience-na.org

San Diego

Email: sandiego@happy-science.org

San Francisco

525 Clinton Street
Redwood City, CA 94062
Phone/Fax: 650-363-2777
Email: sf@happy-science.org
website: sanfrancisco.happyscience-na.org

Florida

12210 N 56th Street
Tampa, FL 33617
Phone:813-914-7771
Fax: 813-914-7710
Email: florida@happy-science.org
website: florida.happyscience-na.org

New Jersey

725 River Road, Suite 200
Edgewater, NJ 07025
Phone: 201-313-0127
Fax: 201-313-0120
Email: nj@happy-science.org
website: newjersey.happyscience-na.org

Atlanta

1874 Piedmont Ave. NE
Suite 360-C
Atlanta, GA 30324
Phone: 404-892-7770
Email: atlanta@happy-science.org
website: atlanta.happyscience-na.org

Hawaii

1221 Kapiolani Blvd., Suite 920
Honolulu, HI 96814
Phone: 808-591-9772
Fax: 808-591-9776
Email: hi@happy-science.org
website: hawaii.happyscience-na.org

Kauai

4504 Kukui Street
Dragon Building Suite 21
P. O. Box 1060
Kapaa, HI 96746
Phone: 808-822-7007
Fax: 808-822-6007
Email: kauai-hi@happy-science.org
website: www.happyscience-kauai.org

Toronto

323 College Street,
Toronto ON M5T 1S2
Canada
Phone/Fax: 1-416-901-3747
Email: toronto@happy-science.org
website: happyscience-na.org

Vancouver

#212-2609 East 49th Avenue
Vancouver, V5S 1J9
Canada
Phone: 1-604-437-7735
Fax: 1-604-437-7764
Email: vancouver@happy-science.org
website: happyscience-na.org

INTERNATIONAL

Tokyo

1-6-7 Togoshi
Shinagawa, Tokyo, 142-0041
Japan
Phone: 81-3-6384-5770
Fax: 81-3-6384-5776
Email: tokyo@happy-science.org
website: www.happy-science.org

London

3 Margaret Street,
London, W1W 8RE
United Kingdom
Phone: 44-20-7323-9255
Fax: 44-20-7323-9344
Email: eu@happy-science.org
website: www.happyscience-uk.org

Sydney

516 Pacific Hwy
Lane Cove North,
2066 NSW
Australia
Phone: 61-2-9411-2877
Fax: 61-2-9411-2822
Email: aus@happy-science.org
website: www.happyscience.org.au

Brazil Headquarters

Rua. Domingos de Morais 1154,
Vila Mariana, Sao Paulo, CEP 04009-002
Brazil
Phone: 55-11-5088-3800
Fax: 55-11-5088-3806
Email: sp@happy-science.org
website: www.cienciadafelicidade.com.br

Seoul

162-17 Sadang3-dong
Dongjak-gu, Seoul, Korea
Phone: 82-2-3478-8777
Fax: 82-2-3478-9777
Email: korea@happy-science.org
website: www.happyscience-korea.org

Taipei

No. 89, Lane 155, Dunhua N. Road
Songshan District
Taipei City 105
Taiwan
Phone: 886-2-2719-9377
Fax: 886-2-2719-5570
Email: taiwan@happy-science.org
website: www.happyscience-tw.org

Kathmandu

Sitapaila -15 kimdol
Ward no -15 Kathmandu
Nepal
Phone: 97-714-272931
Email: nepal@happy-science.org

Uganda

Plot 877 Rubaga Road Kampala
P.O. Box 34130
Kampala, Uganda
Phone: 256-78-4728-601
Email: uganda@happy-science.org
website: www.happyscience-uganda.org

ABOUT IRH PRESS

Founded in 1987, IRH Press is the publishing, broadcast, and film production division of Happy Science. IRH Press currently has offices in Tokyo, New York, Sao Paulo, and Mumbai. The press publishes religious and spiritual books, journals, and magazines, and also operates broadcast and film production enterprises. For more information, visit www.OkawaBooks.com.

OTHER BOOKS BY RYUHO OKAWA

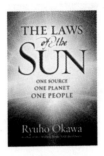

THE LAWS OF THE SUN
One Source, One Planet, One People
ISBN: 978-1-937673-04-8
$24.95 (Hardcover)

IMAGINE IF YOU COULD ASK GOD why He created this world and what spiritual laws He used to shape us—and everything around us. If we could understand His designs and intentions, we could discover what our goals in life should be and whether our actions move us closer to those goals or farther away.

At a young age, a spiritual calling prompted Ryuho Okawa to outline what he innately understood to be universal truths for all humankind. In *The Laws of the Sun*, Okawa outlines these laws of the universe and provides a road map for living one's life with greater purpose and meaning.

In this powerful book, Ryuho Okawa reveals the transcendent nature of consciousness and the secrets of our multidimensional universe and our place in it. By understanding the different stages of love and following the Buddhist Eightfold Path, he believes we can speed up our eternal process of development. *The Laws of the Sun* shows the way to realize true happiness—a happiness that continues from this world through the other.

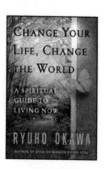

CHANGE YOUR LIFE, CHANGE THE WORLD
A Spiritual Guide to Living Now
ISBN: 978-0-9826985-0-1
$16.95 (Paperback)

MASTER RYUHO OKAWA calls out to people of all nations to remember their true spiritual roots and to build our planet into a united Earth of peace, prosperity, and happiness. With the spiritual wisdom contained in this book, each and every one of us can change our lives and change the world.

THE MOMENT OF TRUTH
Become a Living Angel Today
ISBN: 978-0-9826985-7-0
$14.95 (Paperback)

"To save the seven billion people on Earth, God has countless
angels working constantly, every day, on His behalf."
—Chapter 3

MASTER OKAWA shows that we are essentially spiritual beings
and that our true and lasting happiness is not found within the material world but rather in acts of unconditional and selfless love toward the greater world. These pages reveal God's mind, His mercy,
and His hope that many of us will become living angels that shine
light onto this world.

THE NINE DIMENSIONS
Unveiling the Laws of Eternity
ISBN: 978-0-9826985-6-3
$15.95 (Paperback)

THIS BOOK IS YOUR GATE TO HEAVEN. In this book, Master Okawa shows that God designed this world and the vast, wondrous world of our afterlife as a school with many levels through which our souls learn and grow. This book is a window into the mind of our loving God, who encourages us to grow into greater angels.

SECRETS OF THE EVERLASTING TRUTHS
A New Paradigm for Living on Earth
ISBN: 978-1-937673-10-9
$14.95 (Paperback)

OUR BELIEF IN THE INVISIBLE IS OUR FUTURE. It is our knowledge about the everlasting spiritual laws and our belief in the invisible that will make it possible for us to solve the world's problems and bring our entire planet together. When you discover the secrets in this book, your view of yourself and the world will be changed dramatically and forever.

ALSO BY RYUHO OKAWA

THE SCIENCE OF HAPPINESS
10 Principles for Manifesting Your Divine Nature

THE GOLDEN LAWS
History through the Eyes of the Eternal Buddha

THE STARTING POINT OF HAPPINESS
A Practical and Intuitive Guide to Discovering Love, Wisdom, and Faith

LOVE, NURTURE, AND FORGIVE
A Handbook to Add a New Richness to Your Life

AN UNSHAKABLE MIND
How to Overcome Life's Difficulties

THE ORIGIN OF LOVE
On the Beauty of Compassion

INVINCIBLE THINKING
There Is No Such Thing as Defeat

GUIDEPOSTS TO HAPPINESS
Prescriptions for a Wonderful Life

THE LAWS OF HAPPINESS
The Four Principles for a Successful Life

TIPS TO FIND HAPPINESS
Creating a Harmonious Home for Your Spouse, Your Children, and Yourself

THE PHILOSOPHY OF PROGRESS
Higher Thinking for Developing Infinite Prosperity

THE ESSENCE OF BUDDHA
The Path to Enlightenment

THE CHALLENGE OF THE MIND
A Practical Approach to the Essential Buddhist Teaching of Karma

THE CHALLENGE OF ENLIGHTENMENT
Realize Your Inner Potential